Bibliographies of Modern Authors
ISSN 0749-470X
Number Seven

I0233871

The Work of
KATHERINE KURTZ

An Annotated Bibliography & Guide

by
Boden Clarke
with Mary A. Burgess

R. REGINALD
The Borgo Press
San Bernardino, California □ MCMXCIII

THE BORGO PRESS

Publishers Since 1975
Post Office Box 2845
San Bernardino, CA 92406
United States of America

* * * * * * *

Library of Congress Cataloging-in-Publication Data

Clarke, Boden, 1948-
 The work of Katherine Kurtz : an annotated bibliography & guide / by
Boden Clarke with Mary A. Burgess.
 p. cm. (Bibliographies of modern authors, ISSN 0749-470X ; no. 7)
 Includes index.
 ISBN 0-89370-386-9. — ISBN 0-89370-486-5 (pbk.)
 1. Kurtz, Katherine—Bibliography. 2. Fantastic fiction, American—
Bibliography. I. Burgess, Mary Wickizer, 1938- . II. Title. III. Series:
Bibliographies of modern authors (San Bernardino, Calif.) ; no. 7.
Z8468.64.C55 1993   85-31401
[PS3561.U69]
016.813'54—dc19   CIP

FIRST EDITION

CONTENTS

PRO KATARINA EPISCOPA

PRO MARCO VETERINARIO

PRO DI IMMORTALES!

INTRODUCTION

BRIDGES
An Appreciation of Katherine Kurtz

London Bridge was the first place where I met Katherine Kurtz. It was October of 1974 and the weather was lovely—80-degree temperatures with a brisk breeze which stirred the sands of the field where a battle was ready to begin. The forces were relatively small, only 50 or 60 warriors on each side, armored in a variety of styles as though gathered from across the wide face of medieval Europe. She was a Herald with the invading forces and wore a light colored gown appropriate to the warmth of the day. I wore a houppelande and was the Herald chosen to represent the defenders.

This scene really did take place in our reality, but needs a little explanation. I first *heard* of Katherine in 1970 when her first book appeared on the rack at my local drugstore. Still in high school at that time and not knowing how worthwhile this purchase was to be, I bought it and put in on my shelf of books to be read. By 1973 I had all of the books of that initial trilogy and even had the time to read them. They were good books, and marked her as an author to buy whenever a new novel might appear.

By this time I had gone to college in Arizona and had become involved with the Society for Creative Anachronism, an organization of medievalists, people who were interested in the preservation of a variety of aspects of living history, including music, blacksmithing, combat, and the sense of pageantry of that period in time. Through the grapevine I had heard of a number of authors who were associated with the SCA, and Katherine was on that list. In 1974 the developers of Lake Havasu City, Arizona (who had purchased and relocated London Bridge a few years previously) invited the SCA to have a war at the Bridge in conjunction with the start of a "British Heritage" Festival. This was the background for our first meeting. At that time I only had a chance to briefly introduce myself and tell her of my appreciation for her writing. We were both busy with the war, which was won by the invading forces of the West, who were so impressed by the thorny sands of my home kingdom that they let us keep the Bridge.

During the next two years I met her again at several SCA events in California, and happened to be a guest at a house where she was doing a reading from a work in progress. I learned that she was a costumer, interested in the equestrian arts, and an owner of two horses. When she brought a horse to a subsequent outdoor event, she cut a very dramatic figure in a Tudor riding habit with Scottish accents. She also proved easy to talk with, and I established an occasional correspondence with her as she took on publication of *Deryni Archives*.

My college days ended and I returned to the East Coast, but kept in contact with Katherine. In 1979 I went to my first con, and was delighted to find that she was a guest. A conversation about Deryni magic turned into a brainstorming session in the hotel lobby which lasted until about 3 AM. Ward cubes were employed, a floating crowd grew to as many as 15 or 20 people, and copious notes were made on napkins and the backs of envelopes. Some of the fruits of that session are still appearing in Katherine's books. That con also provided us with the chance to renew our friendship through the sharing of songs, and the chance to talk about her reign as Queen over that same Kingdom of the West which she had represented on the dusty field by London Bridge.

We continued to meet at cons one or twice a year, and usually sat up talking until 3 or 4 AM on a range of subjects which included psychic phenomena versus magic, how they related to religion, reincarnation and how her healing had gone after a horse severely mangled one of her fingers. During this time we continued to write, and Katherine stayed busy by gaining certification as a hypnotist, a skill which also provided useful background for her new writings. She also became a full-time author.

At that time, she began work on her first non-Deryni novel. This gave her an excuse to travel to France and Britain to gather material about World War II and the practitioners of the occult who also fought the war. I had a chance to visit her at home at this time, and we went off to explore the Queen Mary at its permanent berth. The aura of the great ocean liner helped provide background atmosphere for the locked-room mystery on which she was also working, so it counted as a form of research. It was also a great excuse to miss joining a tour group, and sneak through the passages of the ship on our own, giggling like kids and finding our way into several places which we probably shouldn't have visited. That evening was finished off by dining in one of the restaurants on board, an experience which was regretably marred when Katherine contracted a mild form of food poisoning. Later she moved the mystery onto a liner in interstellar space; it was published as *The Legacy of Lehr*.

In the years which followed, Katherine married Scott MacMillan, a long-time friend of hers. With him came his son, Cameron, who is now nearly eighteen years of age. After much soul-searching, the three of them moved to Ireland. There, they were joined by Katherine's charming cat (the Marmalade Bear) as soon as he could clear quarantine. A lengthy quest for a suitable home was successful, and they became the owners of Holybrooke Hall, a manor house located about twenty miles south of Dublin; it was sadly in need of proper restoration, but equipped with its own array of friendly ghosts. Katherine, Scott, and Cameron have poured tremendous quantities of love, sweat, and money into the structure, and it is now the kind of palatial home which most of us harbor secret aspirations of owning...someday.

I had continue to see Katherine at conventions throughout this time, including the Worldcon at Brighton in 1987. I became engaged at that time to Nancy Hanger (who, we learned in a later conversation with Katherine's mother, is probably a third or fourth cousin to Katherine!), and we immediately invited Katherine to participate in our wedding ceremony. She arrived three weeks after my fiancée had a riding accident and broke her back. What was intended to be the visit of a good friend became a mission of mercy as she proved enormously helpful with the final preparations for the wedding. In fact, she was one of six guests who stayed with us the night before the ceremony, and one of two who remained with us for a day or so afterwards (and she seemed much amused by some of what she heard at that time...).

We visited her family twice in 1989, once on our honeymoon, and again in the fall when we all toured together in Scotland following our investiture as companion Chevaliers in the Sovereign Military Order of the Knights of the Temple of Jerusalem, one of three chivalric orders in which Scott and Katherine have been involved for several years (the others being the Knights of St. John and the order of St. Lazarus).

This trip also gave us a new chance to take part in the research for a new book. Katherine had started a collaborative series with Deborah Turner Harris called The Adept. The general theme of these books is the investigation of occult crimes in the modern-day British Isles. Having had a chance to take part in the planning of the fictional theft of the Faery Flag from Dunvegan Castle, and having helped case the joint, I was pleased to see the initial book of the series finally appear in print in 1991.

The restoration work at Holybrooke Hall continues well, and Katherine's human family is owned by three cats. *Deryni Magic* was also published in 1991, and work is well begun on a book about occult influences on the American Revolution. Katherine continues to travel to conventions such as Lunacon, and we have a variety of plans for future visits, on both sides of the Atlantic. A new Deryni book was published at the end of 1992, plus the second volume in the Adept sequence; more are promised for 1993.

Begun tenuously in the desert heat of London Bridge, and continuing to span both the continent and the ocean, the bridge of friendship between Katherine Kurtz and my family has continued to strengthen for over seventeen years. For those who have not yet met her, you will find her to be a warm and interesting human being, with the kind of wide range of interests which encourages fascinating conversations. For those who have not yet read any of her books, I hope that you will have as much pleasure in reading them as I have.

This new guide to her work, a comprehensive annotated bibliography of Katherine Kurtz's novels, stories, and nonfiction, will be welcomed by fans and scholars alike. It is more than just a mass of data, but also includes the longest and most revealing interview with the author ever published, and the reproduction of a little-known essay by Kurtz on the background of the Deryni series. This is the first book ever published about Katherine Kurtz and her fiction; I predict it won't be the last.

—Andrew V. Phillips
Auburn, New Hampshire

A KATHERINE KURTZ CHRONOLOGY

1944 Katherine Irene Kurtz born October 18, 1944 at Coral Gables, Florida, daughter of Fredrick Harry Kurtz (an electronics technician) and Margaret Frances Carter (a school teacher).

1961 Regional semi-finalist in the 1961 Westinghouse Science Talent Search.

1962 Graduates from Coral Gables Senior High School and enters the University of Miami on a full science scholarship.

1964 On October 11th, a week before her twentieth birthday, Kurtz has a remarkably vivid dream which wakes her from a deep sleep; she immediately copies what she can remember of the dream on two 3" x 5" cards. These notes form the basis for the story, "Lords of Sorandor," and later of the entire Deryni universe.

1965 Writes the first pre-Deryni story, "Lords of Sorandor," in October. This includes the concepts and most of the same characters later featured in *Deryni Rising*.

1966 Graduates with a B.S. degree in chemistry from the University of Miami.

1967 Spends a year attending medical school before deciding not to pursue a career as a doctor.

1968 Moves to Southern California to continue graduate studies in English history.

1969 Accepts a position as a Junior Administrative Assistant with the Los Angeles Police Department, initially working in the Narcotics Division (whence came later rumors that she had once been a narcotics officer). Betty Ballantine accepts *Deryni Rising* as the first original title to be featured in the Ballantine Adult Fantasy Series.

1970 Transfers to the Los Angeles Police Academy, where, except for a one-year stint in civilian training, she spends the next eleven years working in various aspects of police officer training as a Senior Training Technician. Kurtz's first professional publication, the novel *Deryni Rising*, is published by Ballantine Books. It has remained in print continuously since its first release.

1971   Obtains her M.A. in medieval English history from the University of California, Los Angeles.

1972   Publishes *Deryni Checkmate*, the second volume in the Chronicles of the Deryni.

1973   The third book in the trilogy, *High Deryni*, is published by Ballantine Books.

1974   Writes *The Legacy of Lehr* for Laser Books, which, however, never publishes it. The book finally appears in extensively rewritten form in 1986.

1976   *Camber of Culdi*, first of the Camber Series, is published by Ballantine.

1977   The author's first published short story, "Swords Against the Marluk," published in *Flashing Swords! #4*. Writes an unpublished and unproduced screenplay (with Don Marrs) based around *Deryni Rising*.

1978   The second Camber novel, *Saint Camber*, is published by Ballantine/Del Rey in cloth, Kurtz's first hardcover publication. "Lords of Sorandor," Kurtz's first attempt at setting down the fantasy world which later became the Deryni Cycle, is published in *The Deryni Archives*, a magazine which Kurtz establishes in this year for fans of the series. *An Hour with Katherine Kurtz*, a lengthy cassette interview, is released by Hourglass Productions.

1980   A lengthy interview with Jeffrey M. Elliot is published in *Fantasy Newsletter*, and in the book, *Fantasy Voices* (1982).

1981   The concluding volume in the Camber Trilogy, *Camber the Heretic*, is published by Del Rey. Resigns her position with the Los Angeles Police Department to become a full-time writer.

1983   The author's first *non*-Deryni book, *Lammas Night*, a twentieth-century story of the supernatural, published by Ballantine Books. Marries Scott Roderick MacMillan, a producer and publisher, on April 9th, and becomes step-mother to nine-year-old Cameron MacMillan.

1984   *The Bishop's Heir*, the first volume in the second Kelson Series, is published in cloth by Ballantine/Del Rey. Publishes the final (tenth) issue of *The Deryni Archives* under her tutelage.

1985   Publishes *The King's Justice*, second in the Kelson Trilogy, and *The Chronicles of the Deryni*, an omnibus volume of the author's first three books.

1986   The concluding volume of the Kelson Trilogy, *The Quest for Saint Camber*, is published by Ballantine/Del Rey in cloth; also released by the same publisher is the author's first collection, *The Deryni Archives*. *The Legacy of Lehr*, Kurtz's first science fiction novel, is published by Walker & Co. in their Millennium series. Sells her home in Sun Valley, CA, and moves to Ireland with her husband and stepson, settling in a castellated 150-year-old manor house in County Wicklow.

1989   Publishes *The Harrowing of Gwynedd*, the first volume of a new Deryni trilogy, The Heirs of Saint Camber, and the tenth of the overall saga.

1990   The author's first science fiction short story, "Manstopper" (with Scott MacMillan), is published in *Total War*.

1991   Ace Books publishes *The Adept* (with Deborah Turner Harris), the first book in a new occult detective series. Also released this year is the grimoire, *Deryni Magic*, from Ballantine Del Rey.

1992   *The Lodge of the Lynx*, the second book in The Adept series (with Deborah Turner Harris), is released by Ace Books. *King Javan's Year*, the second novel in the Heirs of Saint Camber series, and the eleventh Deryni book overall, is published by Ballantine Del Rey.

1993   *The Work of Katherine Kurtz: An Annotated Bibliography & Guide*, the first comprehensive bibliography of the author's publications, is issued by Borgo Press. *The Templar Treasure*, third in the Adept Series (with Deborah Turner Harris), is published by Ace Books.

A.

BOOKS

A1. *Deryni Rising.* The Chronicles of the Deryni, Volume I. New York: Ballantine Books, August 1970, xiv+271 p., paper, novel (ISBN 0-345-01981-4), 95¢. Introduction by Lin Carter (dropped in all later printings). Cover art by Bob Pepper. [fantasy novel]

ab. New York: Ballantine Books, November 1974 (2nd printing), 271 p., paper (ISBN 0-345-24495-8), $1.50. Cover art by Alan Mardon.

ac. New York: Ballantine Books, February 1976 (3rd printing), 271 p., paper (ISBN 0-345-25290-X), $1.95. Cover art by Alan Mardon.

ad. New York: Ballantine Books, October 1976 (4th printing), 271 p., paper (ISBN 0-345-25290-X), $1.95. Cover art by Alan Mardon; cover lettering changed.

ae. New York: Ballantine Books, January 1978 (5th printing), 271 p., paper (ISBN 0-345-25290-X), $1.95. Cover art by Alan Mardon; cover lettering as in 4th printing.

af. New York: Ballantine Books, August 1978 (6th printing), 271 p., paper (ISBN 0-345-27599-3), $1.95. Cover art by Alan Mardon; cover lettering as in 4th printing.

ag. New York: Ballantine Books, May 1980 (7th printing), 271 p., paper (ISBN 0-345-29105-0), $2.25. Cover art by Darrell Sweet.

ah. New York: Ballantine Books, November 1980 (8th printing), 271 p., paper (ISBN 0-345-29105-0), $2.25. Cover art by Darrell Sweet.

ai. New York: Ballantine Books, September 1981 (9th printing), 271 p., paper (ISBN 0-345-30426-8), $2.75. Cover art by Darrell Sweet.

aj. New York: Ballantine Books, May 1982 (10th printing), 271 p., paper (ISBN 0-345-30426-8), $2.75. Cover art by Darrell Sweet.

ak. New York: Ballantine Books, January 1983 (11th printing), 271 p., paper (ISBN 0-345-30426-8), $2.75. Cover art by Darrell Sweet.

al. New York: Ballantine Books, October 1983 (12th printing), 271 p., paper (ISBN 0-345-30426-8), $2.75. Cover art by Darrell Sweet.

am. New York: Ballantine Books, September 1984 (13th printing), 271 p., paper (ISBN 0-345-31987-7), $2.95. Cover art by Darrell Sweet, with cover medallion added.

an. New York: Ballantine Books, December 1985 (14th printing), 271 p., paper (ISBN 0-345-33604-6), $3.50. Cover art by Darrell Sweet, with cover medallion added.

ao. New York: Ballantine Books, September 1987 (15th printing), 271 p., paper (ISBN 0-345-34763-3), $3.95. Cover art by Darrell Sweet, with cover medallion added.

ap. (16th printing).

aq. (17th printing).

ar. (18th printing).

as. (19th printing).

at. New York: Ballantine Books, May 1990 (20th printing), 271 p., paper (ISBN 0-345-34763-3), $4.95. Cover art by Darrell Sweet, with cover medallion added.

au. (21st printing).

av. (22nd printing).

aw. New York: Ballantine Books, September 1991 (23rd printing), 271 p., paper (ISBN 0-345-34763-3), $4.95. Cover art by Darrell Sweet, with cover medallion added.

b. London: Pan/Ballantine Books, 1973, xiv+271 p., paper (ISBN 0-345-09771-8), £0.40. Includes introduction by Lin Carter and Bob Pepper cover.

c. as: *Dar Geschlecht der Magier*. Band 1 der Deryni-Chronik. München: Wilhelm Heyne Verlag, 1978, 238 p., paper. [German]

d. London: Century Publishing, 1985, 271 p., cloth (ISBN 0-7126-1013-8), £8.95.

db. London: Century Publishing, 1985, 271 p., paper (ISBN 0-7126-0848-6), £2.95.

dc. London: Legend Books, November 1986, 271 p., paper (ISBN 0-09-961940-7), £3.50.

e. as: *L'Ascesa dei Deryni*. Milano: Casa Editrice Nord, 1988, 229 p., trade paper with dust jacket. [Italian]

f. as: *Deryni el Resurgir*. Barcelona: Ediciones B., S.A., Marzo 1991, 257 p., trade paper with dust jacket. [Spanish]

The first of Kurtz's novels establishes the background of the kingdom of Gwynedd and the age-old conflict between human and Deryni, who possess genetically transmitted psychic powers. In the year 1120 King Brion Haldane of Gwynedd is assassinated by Charissa, heir to the pretentions of the Festils, a Deryni dynasty which had ruled the kingdom several hundred years earlier.

Succeeding Brion is his teenage son, King Kelson. Kelson's family, although human, possesses powers similar to those of the Deryni, inherited by each member of the family, and triggered by a religious ceremony which anoints the heir apparent (but which was not performed by Kelson's father).

The young prince is taken in hand by two of Brion's chief advisors, Alaric Morgan, Duke of Corwyn and Father Duncan McLain (both Deryni), who together conduct the ritual that enables Kelson's hereditary abilities. Kelson is declared of age, thwarts an attempt by the presiding Archbishop to have Morgan arrested, and is finally crowned king.

During the ceremony Charissa appears, challenges the boy-king to a duel arcane, and is killed by Kelson during the subsequent battle. As the rite is resumed, Kelson and the Deryni members of his entourage see a vision of Camber of Culdi, ancient patron saint of the Deryni.

In structure and execution the most primitive of Kurtz's novels, *Deryni Rising* nonetheless fires the imagination, and establishes the foundations of a carefully structured fantasy kingdom.

SECONDARY SOURCES AND REVIEWS:

1. *Books & Bookmen* 18 (April, 1973): 141.
2. Christopher, Joe. *Riverside Quarterly* 5 (July, 1971): 60-62.
3. Holdom, Lynne. *Capsule Reviews*. Lake Jackson, TX: Joanne Burger, 1977, paper, p. 23.
4. Slater, Ian. *Fantasiae* 1 (September, 1973): 9-10; (November, 1973): 8-9; and (December, 1973): 9-10. A three-part critique of the first Deryni trilogy, the first detailed examination of Kurtz's fiction.
5. Stableford, Brian. *The Deryni Trilogy*, in *Survey of Modern Fantasy Literature*, edited by Frank N. Magill. Englewood Cliffs, NJ: Salem Press, 1983, cloth, Vol. 1, p. 360-365.
6. Tymn, Marshall B., Kenneth J. Zahorski, and Robert H. Boyer. "Kurtz, Katherine. *Deryni Rising*," in *Fantasy Literature: A Core Collection and Reference Guide*. New York & London: R. R. Bowker Co., 1979, cloth, p. 101.
7. Waggoner, Diana. "Kurtz, Katherine, 1944- . *Deryni Rising*," in *The Hills of Faraway: A Guide to Fantasy*. New York: Atheneum, 1978, cloth, p. 213.

A2.   *Deryni Checkmate.* Volume II in the Chronicles of the Deryni. New York: Ballantine Books, May 1972, xii+302 p., paper (ISBN 0-345-02598-9), $1.25. Introduction by Lin Carter (dropped in all later printings). Cover art by Bob Pepper. [fantasy novel]

ab.   New York: Ballantine Books, May 1972 (2nd printing), 302 p., paper (ISBN 0-345-24496-6), $1.50. Cover art by Alan Mardon.
ac.   New York: Ballantine Books, November 1976 (3rd printing), 302 p., paper (ISBN 0-345-25291-8), $1.95. Cover art by Alan Mardon.

ad. New York: Ballantine Books, January 1977 (4th printing), 302 p., paper (ISBN 0-345-27102-5), $1.95. Cover art by Alan Mardon, with cover lettering changed.

ae. New York: Ballantine Books, January 1978 (5th printing), 302 p., paper (ISBN 0-345-27102-5), $1.95. Cover art by Alan Mardon, with cover lettering and cover color changed.

af. New York: Ballantine Books, November 1978 (6th printing), 302 p., paper (ISBN 0-345-27102-5), $1.95. Cover art by Alan Mardon, with cover lettering changed and cover color changed a second time.

ag. New York: Ballantine Books, May 1980 (7th printing), 302 p., paper (ISBN 0-345-29224-3), $2.25. Cover art by Darrell Sweet.

ah. New York: Ballantine Books, March 1981 (8th printing), 302 p., paper (ISBN 0-345-29224-3), $2.25. Cover art by Darrell Sweet.

ai. New York: Ballantine Books, November 1981 (9th printing), 302 p., paper (ISBN 0-345-30593-0), $2.75. Cover art by Darrell Sweet.

aj. New York: Ballantine Books, October 1982 (10th printing), 302 p., paper (ISBN 0-345-30593-0), $2.75. Cover art by Darrell Sweet.

ak. New York: Ballantine Books, June 1983 (11th printing), 302 p., paper (ISBN 0-345-30593-0), $2.75. Cover art by Darrell Sweet.

al. New York: Ballantine Books, March 1984 (12th printing), 302 p., paper (ISBN 0-345-31791-2), $2.95. Cover art by Darrell Sweet, with cover medallion added.

am. New York: Ballantine Books, October 1985 (13th printing), 302 p., paper (ISBN 0-345-31791-2), $2.95. Cover art by Darrell Sweet, with cover medallion added.

an. New York: Ballantine Books, December 1985 (14th printing), 302 p., paper (ISBN 0-345-31791-2), $2.95. Cover art by Darrell Sweet, with cover medallion added.

ao. (15th printing).

ap. New York: Ballantine Books, September 1987 (16th printing), 302 p., paper (ISBN 0-345-34764-1), $3.95. Cover art by Darrell Sweet, with cover medallion added.

aq. (17th printing).

ar. (18th printing).

as. New York: Ballantine Books, October 1989 (19th printing), 302 p., paper (ISBN 0-345-34764-1), $3.95. Cover art by Darrell Sweet, with cover medallion added.

at. (20th printing).

au. (21st printing).

av. New York: Ballantine Books, November 1991 (22nd printing), 302 p., paper (ISBN 0-345-34764-1), $4.95. Cover art by Darrell Sweet, with cover medallion added.

b. London: Pan/Ballantine Books, 1973, xiii+302 p., paper (ISBN 0-345-09772-6), £0.40. Includes introduction by Lin Carter and Bob Pepper cover.

c. as: *Die Zauberfürsten*. Band 2 der Deryni-Chronik. München: Wilhelm Heyne Verlag, 1978, 286 p., paper. Includes map. [German]

d. London: Century Publishing, 1985, 302 p., trade paper (ISBN 0-7126-0849-4), £2.95.

db. London: Century Publishing, 1986, 302 p., cloth (ISBN 0-7126-1012-X), £8.95.

dc. London: Legend, December 1989, 302 p., mass market paper (ISBN 0-09-961950-4), £3.50.

e. as: *La Sfida dei Deryni*. Milano: Casa Editrice Nord, 1989, 266 p., trade paper with dust jacket. [Italian]

f. as: *Deryni Jaque Mate*. Barcelona: Ediciones B., S.A., Mayo 1991, 293 p., trade paper with dust jacket. [Spanish]

In the second novel of the first Deryni trilogy, Duke Alaric Morgan, the most prominent Deryni in all Gwynedd, faces insurrection from rebels and interdiction and excommunication by the Church as the result of the ongoing power struggle between Archbishop Loris and the young King Kelson.

Kelson gathers a few of his close supporters and rushes to Corwyn. The book ends with the crisis building, the leaders of the Church beginning to split into two factions (one supporting the king, one following Loris), and Kelson trying to keep his kingdom from disintegrating into pro- and anti-Deryni cliques.

Deryni Checkmate shows Kurtz growing in her ability to create fictional "history," with the culture and characters of her world being carefully framed within a socio-political universe that seems real.

SECONDARY SOURCES AND REVIEWS:

1. *Books & Bookmen* 18 (April, 1973): 141.
2. Burns, S. *Son of WSFA Journal* no. 68 (September, 1972): 9.
3. del Rey, Lester. *Worlds of If* 21 (July/August, 1972): 140.
4. Fredstrom, B. *Luna Monthly* no. 45 (February, 1973): 24.
5. Holdom, Lynne. *Capsule Reviews*. Lake Jackson, TX: Joanne Burger, 1977, paper, p. 23.
6. *Kliatt Paperback Book Guide* 6 (September, 1972): 27.
7. *Publishers Weekly* 201 (April 10, 1972): 60.
8. Slater, Ian. *Fantasiae* 1 (September, 1973): 9-10; (November, 1973): 8-9; and (December, 1973): 9-10. A three-part critique of the first Deryni trilogy.
9. Stableford, Brian. "*The Deryni Trilogy*," in *Survey of Modern Fantasy Literature*, edited by Frank N. Magill. Englewood Cliffs, NJ: Salem Press, 1983, cloth, Vol. 1, p. 360-365.
10. Tymn, Marshall B., Kenneth J. Zahorski, and Robert H. Boyer. "Kurtz, Katherine. *Deryni Checkmate*," in *Fantasy Literature: A*

Core Collection and Reference Guide. New York & London: R.
R. Bowker Co., 1979, cloth, p. 101-102.

11. Waggoner, Diana. "Kurtz, Katherine, 1944- . *Deryni Checkmate,"*
in *The Hills of Faraway: A Guide to Fantasy.* New York:
Atheneum, 1978, cloth, p. 213.

A3. *High Deryni.* Volume III of the Deryni Chronicle. New York: Ballantine
Books, September 1973, xiv+369 p., paper (ISBN 0-345-23485-5),
$1.25. Introduction by Lin Carter (dropped in all later printings). Cover
art by Alan Mardon. [fantasy novel]

ab. New York: Ballantine Books, November 1974 (2nd printing), 369 p., paper (ISBN 0-345-24497-4), $1.50. Cover art by Alan Mardon, with
cover frame and lettering changed.

ac. New York: Ballantine Books, June 1976 (3rd printing), 369 p., paper
(ISBN 0-345-25626-3), $1.95. Cover art by Alan Mardon, with cover
frame and lettering changed.

ad. New York: Ballantine Books, November 1977 (4th printing), 369 p., paper (ISBN 0-345-27113-0), $1.95. Cover art by Alan Mardon, with
cover frame changed and lettering changed a second time.

ae. New York: Ballantine Books, May 1978 (5th printing), 369 p., paper
(ISBN 0-345-27113-0), $1.95. Cover art by Alan Mardon, with cover
frame changed and lettering changed a second time, and cover border al-
tered.

af. New York: Ballantine Books, January 1980 (6th printing), 369 p., paper
(ISBN 0-345-28614-6), $2.25. Cover art by Darrell Sweet.

ag. New York: Ballantine Books, September 1980 (7th printing), 369 p., paper (ISBN 0-345-28614-6), $2.25. Cover art by Darrell Sweet.

ah. New York: Ballantine Books, June 1981 (8th printing), 369 p., paper
(ISBN 0-345-30278-8), $2.75. Cover art by Darrell Sweet.

ai. New York: Ballantine Books, March 1982 (9th printing), 369 p., paper
(ISBN 0-345-30745-3), $2.95. Cover art by Darrell Sweet, with cover
lettering changed.

aj. New York: Ballantine Books, April 1983 (10th printing), 369 p., paper
(ISBN 0-345-30745-3), $2.95. Cover art by Darrell Sweet, with cover
lettering changed.

ak. New York: Ballantine Books, November 1983 (11th printing), 369 p., paper (ISBN 0-345-30745-3), $2.95. Cover art by Darrell Sweet, with
cover lettering changed.

al. New York: Ballantine Books, July 1985 (12th printing), 369 p., paper
(ISBN 0-345-33140-0), $3.50. Cover art by Darrell Sweet, with cover
lettering changed, and cover medallion added.

am. (13th printing).

an. (14th printing).

A. BOOKS

ao. New York: Ballantine Books, September 1987 (15th printing), 369 p., paper (ISBN 0-345-34766-8), $3.95. Cover art by Darrell Sweet, with cover lettering changed, and cover medallion added.

ap. New York: Ballantine Books, September 1988 (16th printing), 369 p., paper (ISBN 0-345-34766-8), $3.95. Cover art by Darrell Sweet, with cover lettering changed, and cover medallion added.

b. as: *Eine Deryni-König*. Band 3 der Deryni-Chronik. München: Wilhelm Heyne Verlag, 1978, 412 p., paper. Includes map. [German]

c. London: Century Publishing, 1985, 369 p., trade paper (ISBN 0-7126-0740-4), £2.95.

cb. London: Century Publishing, 1985, 369 p., cloth (ISBN 0-7126-9499-4), £9.95.

cc. London: Legend, 1990, 369 p., mass market paper (ISBN 0-09-961930-X), £3.99.

d. as: *Il Signore dei Deryni*. Milano: Casa Editrice Nord, 1989, 404 p., trade paper with dust jacket. [Italian]

e. as: *La Grandeza de los Deryni*. Barcelona: Ediciones B., S.A., 1991, [300] p., trade paper with dust jacket. [Spanish]

In the culminating volume of The Chronicles of the Deryni, the boy king Kelson must confront multiple crises, as the Church splits into two factions, one supporting his enemies; and Wencit, Deryni King of the neighboring country of Torenth, prepares a massive invasion force designed to split Gwynedd in two. Interwoven into these narrative strands are Kelson's coming of age, and the question of the ultimate fate of the Deryni race.

In the end, Archbishop Loris, who would resume wholesale persecution of the Deryni, is defeated and deposed, and replaced with a Kelson supporter. With most of the spiritual and temporal forces of the kingdom united behind him, Kelson and his army proceed to a final confrontation with the Torenth monarch. King Wencit is defeated and killed by the treachery of one of his own lords. Gwynedd is restored to the sane and stable rule of a king who combines the best traits of human and Deryni in his veins, and who seems destined to bring a measure of tolerance and wisdom to his much-buffetted realm.

SECONDARY SOURCES AND REVIEWS:

1. D'Ammassa, Don. *WSFA Journal* no. 83 (April, 1974): R10-R11.
2. del Rey, Lester. *Worlds of If* 22 (January/February, 1974): 130-131.
3. Holdom, Lynne. *Capsule Reviews*. Lake Jackson, TX: Joanne Burger, 1977, paper, p. 23.
4. *Publishers Weekly* 204 (June 19, 1973): 48.
5. Slater, Ian. *Fantasiae* 1 (September, 1973): 9-10; (November, 1973): 8-9; and (December, 1973): 9-10. A three-part critique of the first Deryni trilogy.

6. Stableford, Brian. *"The Deryni Trilogy,"* in *Survey of Modern Fantasy Literature*, edited by Frank N. Magill. Englewood Cliffs, NJ: Salem Press, 1983, cloth, Vol. 1, p. 360-365.

7. Tymn, Marshall B., Kenneth J. Zahorski, and Robert H. Boyer. "Kurtz, Katherine. *High Deryni,"* in *Fantasy Literature: A Core Collection and Reference Guide*. New York & London: R. R. Bowker Co., 1979, cloth, p. 102-103.

8. Waggoner, Diana. "Kurtz, Katherine, 1944- . *High Deryni,"* in *The Hills of Faraway: A Guide to Fantasy*. New York: Atheneum, 1978, cloth, p. 213.

A4. **Camber of Culdi.** Volume I in the Legends of Camber of Culdi. New York: Ballantine Books, July 1976, xx+314 p., paper (ISBN 0-345-24590-3), $1.95. LC 76-6977. Cover art by Ted Coombs. [fantasy novel]

ab. New York: Ballantine Books, November 1976 (2nd printing), xx+314 p., paper (ISBN 0-345-24590-3), $1.95. Cover art by Ted Coombs.

ac. New York: Ballantine Books, January 1978 (3rd printing), xx+314 p., paper (ISBN 0-345-27597-7), $1.95. Cover art by Ted Coombs.

ad. New York: Ballantine Books, May 1979 (4th printing), xx+314 p., paper (ISBN 0-345-28559-X), $2.25. Cover art by Darrell Sweet.

ae. New York: Ballantine Books, January 1980 (5th printing), xx+314 p., paper (ISBN 0-345-28559-X), $2.25. Cover art by Darrell Sweet.

af. New York: Ballantine Books, March 1980 (6th printing), xx+314 p., paper (ISBN 0-345-28559-X), $2.25. Cover art by Darrell Sweet.

ag. New York: Ballantine Books, June 1981 (7th printing), xx+314 p., paper (ISBN 0-345-30147-1), $2.50. Cover art by Darrell Sweet, with inset enlarged.

ah. New York: Ballantine Books, November 1981 (8th printing), xx+314 p., paper (ISBN 0-345-30147-1), $2.50. Cover art by Darrell Sweet, with inset enlarged.

ai. New York: Ballantine Books, June 1982 (9th printing), xx+314 p., paper (ISBN 0-345-30855-7), $2.75. Cover art by Darrell Sweet, with inset enlarged and lettering changed.

aj. New York: Ballantine Books, April 1983 (10th printing), xx+314 p., paper (ISBN 0-345-31926-5), $2.95. Cover art by Darrell Sweet, with inset enlarged and lettering changed.

ak. New York: Ballantine Books, October 1983 (11th printing), xx+314 p., paper (ISBN 0-345-31926-5), $2.95. Cover art by Darrell Sweet, with inset enlarged and lettering changed.

al. New York: Ballantine Books, May 1985 (12th printing), xx+314 p., paper (ISBN 0-345-33594-5), $3.50. Cover art by Darrell Sweet, with inset enlarged and lettering changed a second time.

am. New York: Ballantine Books, December 1985 (13th printing), xx+314 p., paper (ISBN 0-345-33594-5), $3.50. Cover art by Darrell Sweet, with inset enlarged and lettering changed a second time.
an. (14th printing).
ao. (15th printing).
ap. New York: Ballantine Books, September 1987 (16th printing), xx+314 p., paper (ISBN 0-345-34767-6), $3.95. Cover art by Darrell Sweet, with inset enlarged and lettering changed a second time.
aq. (17th printing).
ar. (18th printing).
as. (19th printing).
at. (20th printing.
au. New York: Ballantine Books, February 1991 (21st printing), xx+314 p., paper (ISBN 0-345-34767-6), $4.95. Cover art by Darrell Sweet, with inset enlarged and lettering changed a second time.
b. New York: A Del Rey Book, Ballantine Books, 1979, xx+314 p., cloth (ISBN 0-345-28031-8), $8.95. LC 76-6977. Cover art by Ted Coombs.
c. [Garden City, NY: Science Fiction Book Club, 1979], xvii+265 p., cloth. Title page data read: New York: A Del Rey Book, Ballantine Books.
d. as: *Camber von Culdi: Fantasy-Roman*. Erster Band des Frühen Deryni-Zyklus. München: Wilhelm Heyne Verlag, 1979, 319 p., paper. [German]
e. London: Century Publishing, 1985, xx+314 p., trade paper (ISBN 0-7126-0896-6), £2.95.
eb. London: Century Publishing, 1986, ix+309 p., cloth (ISBN 0-7126-9548-6), £10.95.
ec. London: Legend Books, November 1986, ix+309 p., paper (ISBN 0-09-948100-6), £3.95.
f. as: *Camber av Culdi*. Stockholm: Tryckt av Scandbook AB, Falun 1987, 257 p., paper. [Swedish]
g. as: *Camber de Culdi*. Barcelona: Ediciones B., S.A., 1992?, p., trade paper with dust jacket. Unverified. [Spanish]

With her second Deryni sequence Kurtz turns back the historical clock to a period several hundred years prior to the events in the first series. In the year 903 young King Imre rules Gwynedd, the fifth of the Festillic dynasty. Dissolute and power-hungry, the King has decreed a burdensome tax on all free males to finance the construction of a new capital, and has begun a sexual relationship with his sister, Ariella. Disgusted at these antics, Camber MacRorie, Earl of Culdi, former minister to Imre's father and grandfather, seeks to restrain the monarch and his advisers, without success.

Camber's future son-in-law, Rhys Thuryn, discovers that a patient, an eighty-three-year-old man named Daniel Draper, is in reality Prince Aidan, the only surviving child and heir of the last Haldane king of Gwynedd.

Just before he dies, Daniel tells Rhys that his only grandson, Cinhil, had been made a monk twenty years earlier for his own protection. Rhys, Camber, and Camber's priest-son Joram seek out Father Benedictus, as he is now known, remove him from his cloister, release him (most reluctantly) from his vows, marry him to Megan, Camber's ward, and seek to restore him to the throne.

Cinhil gathers his forces, but hesitates to move until his first-born son is killed by one of Imre's minions. The two kings meet in a duel arcane, and Imre is bested, preferring to kill himself rather than submit. Ariella escapes carrying Imre's unborn son, Mark, who will later provide a line of Festillic pretenders (not to become extinct until the death of Charissa in *Deryni Rising*, two hundred years later).

SECONDARY SOURCES AND REVIEWS:

1. Conat, Kathleen. *Lan's Lantern* no. 22 (February, 1987): 77.
2. Flick, H. Jr. *Kliatt Paperback Book Guide* 10 (November, 1976): 81.
3. Holdom, Lynne. *Capsule Reviews*. Lake Jackson, TX: Joanne Burger, 1977, paper, p. 23.
4. MacPherson, W. *Science Fiction Review Monthly* no. 19 (September, 1976): 18.
5. *Publishers Weekly* 209 (May 31, 1976): 197.
6. Slater, Ian. *Fantasiae* 4 (July, 1976): 7-9.
7. Tymn, Marshall B., Kenneth J. Zahorski, and Robert H. Boyer. "Kurtz, Katherine. *Camber of Culdi*," in *Fantasy Literature: A Core Collection and Reference Guide*. New York & London: R. R. Bowker Co., 1979, cloth, p. 103.
8. Wood, Susan. *Delap's F & SF Review* 3 (January, 1977): 19-20.

A5.   *Saint Camber.* Volume II in the Legends of Camber of Culdi. New York: A Del Rey Book, Ballantine Books, October 1978, x+467 p., cloth (ISBN 0-345-27750-3). LC 78-16702. Cover art by Darrell Sweet. [fantasy novel]

  ba. New York: A Del Rey Book, Ballantine Books, September 1979 (1st printing), x+449 p., paper (ISBN 0-345-25952-1), $2.25. Cover art by Darrell Sweet.
  bb. New York: A Del Rey Book, Ballantine Books, November 1980 (2nd printing), x+449 p., paper (ISBN 0-345-25952-1), $2.25. Cover art by Darrell Sweet.
  bc. New York: A Del Rey Book, Ballantine Books, November 1981 (3rd printing), x+449 p., paper (ISBN 0-345-30220-6), $2.75. Cover art by Darrell Sweet, with inset enlarged.

bd. New York: A Del Rey Book, Ballantine Books, July 1982 (4th printing), x+449 p., paper (ISBN 0-345-30862-X), $2.95. Cover art by Darrell Sweet, with inset enlarged and lettering changed.

be. New York: A Del Rey Book, Ballantine Books, March 1983 (5th printing), x+449 p., paper (ISBN 0-345-30862-X), $2.95. Cover art by Darrell Sweet, with inset enlarged and lettering changed.

bf. New York: A Del Rey Book, Ballantine Books, March 1984 (6th printing), x+449 p., paper (ISBN 0-345-30862-X), $2.95. Cover art by Darrell Sweet, with inset enlarged and lettering changed.

bg. New York: A Del Rey Book, Ballantine Books, January 1986 (7th printing), x+449 p., paper (ISBN 0-345-30862-X), $2.95. Cover art by Darrell Sweet, with inset enlarged and lettering changed.

bh. (8th printing).

bi. (9th printing).

bj. New York: A Del Rey Book, Ballantine Books, September 1987 (10th printing), x+449 p., paper (ISBN 0-345-34768-4), $3.95. Cover art by Darrell Sweet, with inset enlarged and lettering changed.

bk. (11th printing).

bl. New York: A Del Rey Book, Ballantine Books, October 1989 (12th printing), x+449 p., paper (ISBN 0-345-34768-4), $4.95. Cover art by Darrell Sweet, with inset enlarged and lettering changed.

bm. New York: A Del Rey Book, Ballantine Books, November 1991 (13th printing), x+449 p., paper (ISBN 0-345-34768-4), $4.95. Cover art by Darrell Sweet, with inset enlarged and lettering changed.

c. as: *Sankt Camber: Fantasy-Roman.* Zweiter Band des Frühen Deryni-Zyklus. München: Wilhelm Heyne Verlag, 1980, 461 p., paper. [German]

d. [Garden City, NY: Science Fiction Book Club, 1981], x+365 p., cloth. Title page copy states: New York: A Del Rey Book, Ballantine Books. Cover painting by Darrell Sweet.

e. London: Century Publishing, 1985, x+449 p., trade paper (ISBN 0-7126-0897-4), £2.95.

eb. London: Century Publishing, September 1986, x+449 p., cloth (ISBN 0-7126-9549-4), £10.95.

ec. London: Legend Books, November 1986, [582] p., paper (ISBN 0-09-948110-3), £4.95.

f. as: *San Camber.* Barcelona: Ediciones B., S.A., 1992?, p., trade paper with dust jacket. Unverified. [Spanish]

In the year 905, six months after the deposition of King Imre and the restoration of the Haldane dynasty in the person of King Cinhil, Camber of Culdi must help organize the monarch's forces to defend Gwynedd against the impending invasion of Ariella, sister to Imre and mother of his son Mark. The two armies meet in a huge battle, which is narrowly won by the forces of Cinhil. However, Father Alister Cullen, the King's close adviser, is slain, although he simultaneously manages to kill Ariella.

Camber and his son Joram discover the bodies shortly after the battle ends, and Camber resolves to assume Alister's place, shapeshifting himself into the priest's outward form, while pretending that it was Camber himself who had been killed. Earl Camber has outlived his usefulness; Alister must continue to live to provide a positive influence on the king and his supporters, to prevent what Camber feels will be an anti-Deryni backlash.

But Cinhil rewards Cullen with a bishopric, and Camber faces a dilemma: he is not a priest, and faces the real possibility of desecrating his new office. Secretly, he arranges for his own ordination by several confidantes in the Church, and thus legally assumes his rank when he is ordained bishop. Camber also begins to gather together responsible surviving members of the Deryni community, founding the Camberian Council, an oversight body of Deryni adepts to police abuses by their fellows.

In the meantime, a brief golden era follows Cinhil's defeat of the Festillic pretenders. The cult of Camber is touted in the land, despite everything that Alister/Camber can do to stop it; and soon Saint Camber is proclaimed, "Defender of Humankind, Kingmaker."

SECONDARY SOURCES AND REVIEWS:

1.   Brown, Charles N. *Isaac Asimov's Science Fiction Magazine* 3 (January, 1979): 16.
2.   Conat, Kathleen. *Lan's Lantern* no. 22 (February, 1987): 77-78.
3.   Flick, H. Jr. *Kliatt Young Adult Paperback Book Guide* 14 (January, 1980): 18.
4.   *Kirkus Reviews* 46 (September 15, 1978): 904.
5.   Niederman, F. *Best Sellers* 39 (November, 1979): 281.
6.   *Publishers Weekly* 214 (September 11, 1978): 77.
7.   Tymn, Marshall B., Kenneth J. Zahorski, and Robert H. Boyer. "Kurtz, Katherine. *Saint Camber*," in *Fantasy Literature: A Core Collection and Reference Guide*. New York & London: R. R. Bowker Co., 1979, cloth, p. 104.
8.   Wood, Susan. *Locus* no. 216 (November, 1978): 8.

A6.   *Camber the Heretic.* Volume III in the Legends of Camber of Culdi. New York: A Del Rey Book, Ballantine Books, November 1981, xi+506 p., paper (ISBN 0-345-27784-8), $2.95. LC 81-66657. Cover art by Darrell Sweet. [fantasy novel]

ab.   New York: A Del Rey Book, Ballantine Books, March 1983 (2nd printing), xi+506 p., paper (ISBN 0-345-27784-8), $2.95. Cover art by Darrell Sweet.

ac. New York: A Del Rey Book, Ballantine Books, March 1983 (3rd printing), xi+506 p., paper (ISBN 0-345-27784-8), $2.95. Cover art by Darrell Sweet.

ad. New York: A Del Rey Book, Ballantine Books, October 1983 (4th printing), xi+506 p., paper (ISBN 0-345-27784-8), $2.95. Cover art by Darrell Sweet.

ae. New York: A Del Rey Book, Ballantine Books, August 1985 (5th printing), xi+506 p., paper (ISBN 0-345-33142-7), $3.50. Cover art by Darrell Sweet, with lettering changed.

af. New York: A Del Rey Book, Ballantine Books, November 1985 (6th printing), xi+506 p., paper (ISBN 0-345-33142-7), $3.50. Cover art by Darrell Sweet, with lettering changed.

ag. (7th printing).

ah. (8th printing).

ai. New York: A Del Rey Book, Ballantine Books, March 1987 (9th printing), xi+506 p., paper (ISBN 0-345-34754-4), $3.95. Cover art by Darrell Sweet, with lettering changed.

aj. New York: A Del Rey Book, Ballantine Books, September 1987 (10th printing), xi+506 p., paper (ISBN 0-345-34754-4), $3.95. Cover art by Darrell Sweet, with lettering changed.

ak. New York: A Del Rey Book, Ballantine Books, October 1988 (11th printing), xi+506 p., paper (ISBN 0-345-34754-4), $3.95. Cover art by Darrell Sweet, with lettering changed.

al. (12th printing).

am. New York: A Del Rey Book, Ballantine Books, April 1991 (13th printing), xi+506 p., paper (ISBN 0-345-34754-4), $4.95. Cover art by Darrell Sweet, with lettering changed.

b. [Garden City, NY: Science Fiction Book Club, 1982], x+491 p., cloth. Title page copy reads: New York: A Del Rey Book, Ballantine Books.

c. as: *Camber der Ketzer: Fantasy-Roman.* Dritter Band des Frühen Deryni-Zyklus. München: Wilhelm Heyne Verlag, 1983, 674 p., paper. [German]

d. London: Legend Books, Arrow, November 1986, xi+506 p., paper (ISBN 0-09-948090-5), £4.50.

db. London: Century Publishing, March 1987, xi+506 p., cloth (ISBN 0-7126-1585-7), £11.95.

e. as: *Camber el Hereje.* Barcelona: Ediciones B., S.A., 1992?, p., trade paper with dust jacket. Unverified. [Spanish]

The year is 917, a decade after the events in *Saint Camber.* King Cinhil is dying, and the human members of the High Council of Gwynedd are plotting to assume power when he dies. The carefully crafted balance between Deryni and human is disintegrating amidst powerful forces of hate and ambition. Only Camber of Culdi, shapeshifted into the body of Bishop Alister, now Chancellor of Gwynedd, can stem the tide of evil.

Before the old king dies, he sets the Haldane magical potential in each of his three surviving sons. Then he expires in Camber's arms. The conspirators are ready: they declare themselves regents, depose Camber from his position as Chancellor, and eventually from his ecclesiastical office, after he has been briefly elected primate Archbishop of Gwynedd. Those bishops supporting tolerance are executed or deposed, and anti-Deryni clerics elected in their places. The pogrom has started.

Soon the Ramos Convention is ratified, outlawing Deryni from all positions of influence, including the priesthood and civil offices. Offenders are executed, and Deryni lords degraded and their lands redistributed. Camber/Alister is himself outlawed.

Trapped in flight with his companion Jebediah, Camber fights off the attack, but his friend is killed. Tired and wounded and without a source of heat in the middle of a winter night, he preserves his body with an ancient spell, knowing that it will trap him halfway between Heaven and earth, but preserve his spirit to continue the long struggle for Deryni-human tolerance.

This is one of Kurtz's best novels, full of pathos and high drama, of emotion and all the higher virtues.

SECONDARY SOURCES AND REVIEWS:

1. Brown, Charles N. *Locus* 14 (December, 1981): 21.
2. Flick, H. Jr. *Kliatt Young Adult Paperback Book Guide* 16 (January, 1982): 21-22.
3. Green, Roland. *Booklist* 78 (November 1, 1981): 355.
4. *Publishers Weekly* 220 (September 25, 1981): 87.
5. Sawyer, A. *Paperback Inferno* no. 64 (February/March, 1987): 6.
6. Sullivan, C. W. *Science Fiction & Fantasy Book Review* n.s. 1 (January/February, 1982): 21-22.

A7.   *Lammas Night.* New York: Ballantine Books, December 1983, 438 p., paper (ISBN 0-345-29516-1), $3.50. LC 83-90784. [supernatural novel]

ab.   (2nd printing).
ac.   (3rd printing).
ad.   (4th printing).
ae.   (5th printing).
af.   (6th printing).
ag.   New York: Ballantine Books, 1991 (7th printing), 438 p., paper (ISBN 0-345-29516-1), $4.95.
b.   London: Severn House, February 1986, 438 p., cloth (ISBN 0-7278-1249-1), £8.95.

A. BOOKS

This was Kurtz's first novel set in modern times, her original title having been *The Lammas Option*. In 1940 Adolf Hitler, having mastered most of Europe, is looking across the English Channel to Great Britain, his last rival for European domination. Not only has he assembled the mightiest war machine the continent has ever seen, but he is also consorting with black mages in an effort to subvert England's will.

John Graham, a colonel of British Intelligence, accepts a unique assignment: to rally witches' covens throughout the Isles, to fight evil with positive magic, and to do what must be done to stop Hitler's invasion of England. In the end, nothing seems to have any effect, until the King's youngest brother, Prince William, Duke of Clarence, offers himself as a sacrifice. In times of crisis only the death of a royal scion—an offering of the sacred king—can halt the forces of evil. Prince William's plane crashes, Hitler abandons his plans, and Britain (and the world) are saved.

This is an interesting departure for Kurtz, with some effective moments, although *Lammas Night* has been the least popular of her fictions in America. The author revived the idea of a council of "good" witches in her Adept series, written with Deborah Turner Harris, with a definite connection between *Lammas Night* and the later books being established in the second novel of that series, *The Lodge of the Lynx* (see A17).

SECONDARY SOURCES AND REVIEWS:

1.   Ann, Julie. ___: 6. Title and date unknown.
2.   Bradley, Marion Zimmer. "Fighting a War with Astrology," in *San Francisco Chronicle* (Jan. 8, 1984): .
3.   Kies, Cosette. *Supernatural Fiction for Teens: 500 Good Paperbacks to Read for Wonderment, Fear, and Fun*. Littleton, CÓ: Libraries Unlimited, 1987, paper, p. 44.
4.   Kies, Cosette. *Supernatural Fiction for Teens: More Than 1300 Good Paperbacks to Read for Wonderment, Fear, and Fun, 2d Edition*. Englewood, CO: Libraries Unlimited, 1992, paper, p. 98.
5.   Sefton, Laurie. "No Prisoners," in *OtherRealms* no. 28 (1991): 38.

A8.   *The Bishop's Heir*. Volume I of the Histories of King Kelson. New York: A Del Rey Book, Ballantine Books, October 1984, xviii+346 p., cloth (ISBN 0-345-31824-2), $10.95. LC 84-4935. Cover art by Darrell Sweet; map by Shelly Shapiro. [fantasy novel]

ba.   New York: A Del Rey Book, Ballantine Books, August 1985 (1st printing), xix+361 p., paper (ISBN 0-345-30097-1), $3.50. Cover art by Darrell Sweet.
bb.   (2nd printing).
bc.   (3rd printing).

bd. New York: A Del Rey Book, Ballantine Books, September 1987 (4th printing), xix+361 p., paper (ISBN 0-345-34761-7), $3.95. Cover art by Darrell Sweet, with title color changed.

c. [Garden City, NY: Science Fiction Book Club, April 1985], ix+300 p., cloth. Title page reads: New York: A Del Rey Book, Ballantine Books.

d. London: Century Publishing, 1985, xviii+345 p., cloth.

db. London: Century Publishing, 1985, xviii+345 p., trade paper (ISBN 0-7126-0935-0), £2.95.

dc. London: Legend Books, April 1986, [368] p., paper (ISBN 0-09-947800-5), £2.95.

e. as: *Das Erbe des Bischofs*. Erster Roman der Geschichte von König Kelson. München: Wilhelm Heyne Verlag, 1989, 527 p., paper. [German]

f. as: *El Heredero del Obispo*. Barcelona: Ediciones B., S.A., 1992?, p., trade paper with dust jacket. Unverified. [Spanish]

The first book of the third trilogy dealing with the history of Gwynedd returns to the "modern" era of King Kelson, taking place two years after the conclusion of *High Deryni*. Ex-primate Edmund Loris, who has been confined since Kelson's assertion of authority in a lonely northern monastery, escapes from captivity, and heads south to the once independent principality of Meara.

There he rallies his forces around the pretender to the Mearan throne, and hoists the flag of rebellion once again. But Kelson manages to capture the younger son and daughter of the Mearan pretender, and returns with them to his capital. He then gives the Mearans an ultimatum: submit by Christmas to the king's authority, or be invaded. In response, Loris executes the legitimate bishop of Meara, and renews his defiance. Kelson proposes to end the rebellion by marrying the Mearan princess, Sidana, who agrees to the union to spare her countrymen further bloodshed. Just as the King and his new Queen complete their vows, Sidana's older brother stabs her with a knife, and she drops dead at Kelson's feet. For the young King of Gwynedd, all roads are now covered in blood.

The "bishop" mentioned in the title is not Loris, but Kelson's friend Duncan, who discovers almost accidentally that the king's squire, Dhugal, is his son by a common-law marriage consummated before Duncan entered the priesthood. The mother died shortly after giving birth, the child being made a ward of his grandfather. The authorities examine the relationship, decide that the marriage was valid, and certify the boy as legal heir to Duncan's title.

SECONDARY SOURCES AND REVIEWS:

1. Bauerle, Diane K. *Fantasy Review* 8 (March, 1985): 23.
2. *Booklist* 86 (January 1, 1990): 905.

3. Cassada, J. *Library Journal* 109 (November 15, 1984): 2163.
4. D'Ammassa, Don. *Science Fiction Chronicle* 8 (May, 1987): 48.
5. Deal, P. *Voice of Youth Advocates* 8 (April, 1985): 55.
6. *Kirkus Reviews* 52 (September 1, 1984): 829.
7. *Kliatt Young Adult Paperback Book Guide* 19 (October, 1985): 3-4.
8. *Publishers Weekly* 226 (September 21, 1984): 92.
9. Storb, B. *School Library Journal* 31 (January, 1985): 92.

A9. *The Chronicles of the Deryni: Deryni Rising, Deryni Checkmate, High Deryni.* Garden City, NY: Nelson Doubleday, April 1985, 752 p., cloth. [fantasy omnibus]

An omnibus book club edition containing the first three volumes of the Deryni Cycle.
CONTENTS: *Deryni Rising* (1970; see A1); *Deryni Checkmate* (1972; see A2); *High Deryni* (1973; see A3).

A10. *The King's Justice.* Volume II of the Histories of King Kelson. New York: A Del Rey Book, Ballantine Books, November 1985, xxv+337 p., cloth (ISBN 0-345-31825-0), $16.95. LC 85-6198. Cover art by Darrell Sweet; map by Shelly Shapiro. [fantasy novel]

ba. New York: A Del Rey Book, Ballantine Books, August 1986 (1st printing), xxiv+322 p., paper (ISBN 0-345-33196-6), $3.50. Cover art by Darrell Sweet.
bb. (2nd printing).
bc. New York: A Del Rey Book, Ballantine Books, September 1987 (3rd printing), xxiv+322 p., paper (ISBN 0-345-34762-5), $3.95. Cover art by Darrell Sweet.
c. [Garden City, NY: Science Fiction Book Club, 1985], ix+303 p., cloth. Title page reads: New York: A Del Rey Book, Ballantine Books.
d. London: Legend, Arrow Books, April 1986, xxv+336 p., trade paper (ISBN 0-09-945870-8), £2.95.
db. London: Century Publishing, June 1986, xxv+336 p., cloth (ISBN 0-7126-9509-5), £9.95.
e. as: *Die Gerechtigkeit des Königs.* Zweiter Roman der Geschichte von König Kelson. München: Wilhelm Heyne Verlag, 1989, 526 p., paper. [German]
f. as: *La Justicia del Rey.* Barcelona: Ediciones B., S.A., 1992?, p., trade paper with dust jacket. Unverified. [Spanish]

The original manuscript title for this book was *The Return of the Queen.*

In this direct sequel to *The Bishop's Heir*, King Kelson pursues the military campaign against the rebel forces in Meara. In preparation for his prolonged absence, he activates the magical powers of his uncle, Prince Nigel, who will remain behind as regent to protect the realm. But the enemy will seemingly not come to grips, as Kelson's army encounters only small raiding parties from the Mearan forces. The main army has been secretly moved to attack Duncan's troops in the mountainous north. Duncan's force is overwhelmed, and Duncan himself taken prisoner.

As Kelson rides to the rescue, Bishop Duncan is tortured to reveal the whereabouts of the main Gwynedd army. The Mearans have tarried too long, and Kelson's own men attack even as Archbishop Loris prepares to burn Duncan at the stake. The Mearans are routed, Loris captured, and Duncan saved. Loris and the Mearan pretenders are executed, and the king's justice restored to the land.

SECONDARY SOURCES AND REVIEWS:

1. *Best Sellers* 45 (March, 1986): 446.
2. *Booklist* 86 (January 1, 1990): 905.
3. Cassada, J. *Library Journal* 110 (November 15, 1985): 111-112.
4. D'Ammassa, Don. *Science Fiction Chronicle* 8 (May, 1987): 48.
5. Ducharme, Michael J. *Fantasy Review* 9 (January, 1986): 20.
6. Green, Roland. *Booklist* 82 (October 1, 1985): 153.
7. *Kirkus Reviews* 53 (October 1, 1985): 1049-1050.
8. Major, Joseph T. "Justice in Peace," in *Fosfax* no. 101 (March, 1986): 13.
9. *School Library Journal* 32 (February, 1986): 103.
10. *Science Fiction Review* 15 (February, 1986): 50.

A11. *The Deryni Archives.* New York: A Del Rey Book, Ballantine Books, August 1986, 325 p., paper (ISBN 0-345-32678-4), $3.95. LC 86-90861. Cover art by Darrell Sweet; map by Shelly Shapiro. [fantasy collection]

ab. (2nd printing).
ac. (3rd printing).
ad. (4th printing).
ae. New York: A Del Rey Book, Ballantine Books, August 1986 (5th printing), 325 p., paper (ISBN 0-345-32678-4), $3.95. Cover art by Darrell Sweet.
af. New York: A Del Rey Book, Ballantine Books, October 1988 (6th printing), 325 p., paper (ISBN 0-345-32678-4), $3.95. Cover art by Darrell Sweet.

b. [Garden City, NY: Science Fiction Book Club, 1986], 209 p., cloth. Title page reads: New York: A Del Rey Book, Ballantine Books. Cover art by Daniel R. Horne.
c. London: A Legend Book, 1988, 325 p., trade paper.
e. as: *Die Deryni-Archiv*. München: Wilhelm Heyne Verlag, 1989?, p., paper. Unverified. [German]

A collection of stories set in the Deryni world, many of them previously published. Kurtz also contributed new introductions to each of the individual stories.

CONTENTS: Introduction; "Catalyst: Fall, 888" (1985; see B8); "Healer's Song: August 1, 914" (1980; see B3); "Vocation: December 24, 977" (1983; see B7); "Bethane: Summer, 1100" (1982; see B6); "The Priesting of Arilan: August 1, 1104-February 2, 1105" (1986; see B9); "Legacy: June 21, 1105" (1981; see B4); "The Knighting of Derry: May, 1115" (1986; see B10); "Trial: Spring, 1118" (1986; see B11); Appendix I: Index of Characters; Appendix II: Index of Place Names; Appendix III: A Partial Chronology for the Eleven Kingdoms; Appendix IV: Literary Origins of the Deryni, including: "How the Series Began," "The Dream That Became Deryni" (1986; see B12), "Lords of Sorandor" (1978; see B2), "Precis of *Deryni Rising*" (1986; see B13), "Submission Outline for *Deryni Rising*" (1986; see B14).

The early story, "Swords Against the Marluk" (1977; see B1) was omitted because it will form the basis for a later trilogy of novels on Duncan McLain and Alaric Morgan. For individual descriptions of these tales, see their listings in the Short Fiction chapter of this book.

SECONDARY SOURCES AND REVIEWS:

1. Bispham, L. *Paperback Inferno* no. 73 (August/September, 1988): 9.
2. *Booklist* 82 (August, 1986): 1667.
3. *Emergency Librarian* 14 (March, 1987): 49.
4. *Library Journal* 111 (August, 1986): 174.
5. McDonald, P. *Interzone* no. 24 (Summer, 1988): 60.
6. O'Brien, Terry. *Lan's Lantern* no. 22 (February, 1987): 78-79.
7. *School Library Journal* 33 (November, 1986): 116.
8. *Voice of Youth Advocates* 9 (December, 1986): 238.

A12. *The Quest for Saint Camber.* Volume III in the Histories of King Kelson. New York: A Del Rey Book, Ballantine Books, November 1986, xxvi+435 p., cloth (ISBN 0-345-31826-9), $16.95. LC 86-8249. Cover art by Darrell Sweet; map by Shelly Shapiro. [fantasy novel] ba. New York: A Del Rey Book, Ballantine Books, September 1987 (1st printing), xxvi+449 p., paper (ISBN 0-345-30099-8), $3.95. Cover art by Darrell Sweet.

c. [Garden City, NY: Science Fiction Book Club, 1986], 401 p., cloth. Title page reads: New York: A Del Rey Book, Ballantine Books. Cover art by Darrell Sweet.

d. London: Century Publishing, 1987, xxvi+435 p., cloth (ISBN 0-7126-1616-0), £11.95.

db. London: Century Publishing, 1987, xxvi+435 p., trade paper.

dc. London: Arrow Books, May 1987, xxvi+435 p., paper (ISBN 0-09-950360-3), £3.95.

e. as: *Die Suche nach Sankt Camber*. Dritter Roman der Geschichte von König Kelson. München: Wilhelm Heyne Verlag, 1989, 719 p., paper. [German]

f. as: *La Búsqueda de San Camber*. Barcelona: Ediciones B., S.A., 1992?, p., trade paper with dust jacket. Unverified. [Spanish]

One of the more interesting books in the Deryni cycle, *Quest* begins at a quieter pace than its predecessors. In the aftermath of the Mearan campaign, order is being restored to the kingdom by young King Kelson, who has just turned eighteen. It is time, say his advisers, that he think of marrying, and young Lady Rothana, whom he rescued in *The King's Justice*, seems both compatible and willing. First, however, Kelson is determined to discover what he can of the relics of Saint Camber, a semi-mythical figure from several centuries before, and he proceeds on a quest into the further reaches of the realm. During a rainstorm, he and his foster-brother, Dhugal, are swept off a muddy bank into a river, and presumably killed. Kelson's uncle Nigel becomes regent, but Nigel's oldest son, Prince Conall, who has secretly been brought to his powers by a prominent Deryni, suddenly assumes power by putting a psychic lock on his father.

In the meantime, Kelson and Dhugal awake in the bowels of the earth, having been swept into an underground passageway, and left with bruises and other serious injuries. They gradually recover and work their way through a maze of caverns, fighting starvation as well as the ever-present darkness. They finally emerge on the other side of the mountains amidst a cult of Camber-worshippers. They escape and return to Rhemuth, where Kelson confronts Conall, defeats him, has the pretender executed, and restores Nigel to health. But the beautiful Rothana, who has legally become Conall's wife (and is pregnant with his son) is lost to Kelson forever.

SECONDARY SOURCES AND REVIEWS:

1. *Booklist* 82 (July, 1986): 1562.
2. *Booklist* 86 (January 1, 1990): 905.
3. *Christian Science Monitor* 80 (January 13, 1988): 20.

4. *Fantasy Review* 9 (December, 1986): 36.
5. *Kirkus Reviews* 54 (August 1, 1986): 1161.
6. *Library Journal* 111 (September 15, 1986): 102.
7. Major, Joseph T. "In Search of King Kelson," in *Fosfax* no. 103 (October, 1986): 10.
8. O'Brien, Terry. *Lan's Lantern* no. 22 (February, 1978): 78.
9. *Publishers Weekly* 230 (August 8, 1986): 58.
10. *School Library Journal* 33 (December, 1986): 126.

A13. *The Legacy of Lehr.* New York: Millennium, A Byron Preiss Book, Walker & Co., December 1986, 235 p., cloth (ISBN 0-8027-6661-7), $15.95. LC 86-15899. Illustrations and cover art by Michael William Kaluta. [science fiction novel]

b. New York: A Byron Preiss Book, Avon, February 1988, 215 p., paper (ISBN 0-380-70454-4), $3.50. Cover art by Joe DeVito.

c. London: Hutchinson, November 1988, [144] p., cloth (ISBN 0-09-173761-3), £6.95.

cb. London: Beaver Books, November 1989, [240] p., paper (ISBN 0-09-960960-6), £2.99.

This science-fiction mystery was originally written for Laser Books (see H2), but was cancelled when the publisher discontinued its line. Kurtz extensively reworked the novel for the Millennium series.

The luxury space cruiser *Valkyrie* is diverted from her regular run to pick up four large alien "cats" with psychic powers. Mather Seton and Wallis Hamilton, the husband-and-wife team in charge of the aliens, find themselves investigating a series of bizarre murders in which the cats are implicated, although both scientists are convinced the creatures have never left their specially-constructed pens. Their search for the real killer leads nowhere, until one of the cats is killed in a way that is clearly impossible. The mystery is solved, the remaining cats are saved, and the stage is set for further adventures of this likable couple.

A fast-moving, thoroughly entertaining space opera, framed with nine black-and-white Kaluta drawings, this is the author's first published work of science fiction.

SECONDARY SOURCES AND REVIEWS:

1. Betancourt, John Gregory. *Weird Tales* 50 (Spring, 1988): 141.
2. *Book Report* 5 (March, 1987): 31.
3. *Booklist* 83 (November 15, 1986): 502.
4. Byrne, Andrea. *Seventeen* (March, 1987): .
5. D'Ammassa, Don. *Science Fiction Chronicle* 9 (August, 1988): 52.

6. *Fantasy Review* 9 (December, 1986): 40.
7. *Library Journal* 111 (November 15, 1986): 113.
8. Miles, M. *Voice of Youth Advocates* 10 (April, 1987): 38.
9. O'Brien, Terry. *Lan's Lantern* no. 22 (February, 1987): 79.
10. *Publishers Weekly* 230 (September 26, 1986): 69.
11. Von Rospach, Chuq. "Words of Wizdom." *OtherRealms* no. 11 (1986): 21-22.

A14. *The Harrowing of Gwynedd.* Volume I of the Heirs of Saint Camber. New York: A Del Rey Book, Ballantine Books, February 1989, xii+384 p., cloth (ISBN 0-345-33259-8), $17.95. LC 88-7414. Cover art by Michael Herring. An erratum page correcting the genealogical chart on page 381 was also included. [fantasy novel]

ba. New York: A Del Rey Book, Ballantine Books, September 1989 (1st printing), xii+432 p., paper (ISBN 0-345-36314-0), paper, $4.95.
c. London: Century Publishing, December 1989, xii+384 p., cloth (ISBN 0-7126-3495-9), £12.95.
cb. London: Century Publishing, December 1989, xii+384 p., trade paper (ISBN 0-7126-3500-9), £6.95.
cc. London: Legend, 1990, xii+384 p., trade paper (ISBN 0-09-971070-6).
d. as: *El Horror de Gwynedd.* Barcelona: Ediciones B., S.A., 1992?, p., trade paper with dust jacket. Unverified. [Spanish]

The initial volume in Kurtz's latest trilogy returns to the early history of Gwynedd, directly following the events of *Camber the Heretic.* In the year 918 the regents for young King Alroy are tightening their grip on the country, and beginning their systematic persecution of anyone associated with the Deryni race. Camber's body lies incorruptible in its crypt; somehow he managed as he lay dying to weave a spell that would preserve his spirit on Earth, there to influence events into the indefinite future. Camber, previously declared a saint, has now been labelled "heretic" by Archbishop Hubert and his rabid supporters.

Camber's daughter Evaine is determined to find a way to bring her father's spirit back to earth, and reunite it with his body. To this end she begins searching for an obscure occult manuscript, the *Codex Orini*, which allegedly provides this knowledge to those willing to risk their own lives in its pursuit. She decides to take that risk, and with the aid of her brother, Joram, passes beyond the gates of Heaven. Suddenly she realizes that the spell her father wove is terribly flawed, that it has trapped him between the worlds, and that to release him to move freely she must use her own body as a channel for the immense energies required. This she does, sacrificing herself for the future good of her people.

A. BOOKS

Perhaps the most moving volume in the entire Deryni cycle, *Harrowing* reflects a new maturity in Kurtz's fiction. The characters are real and believable, their actions one with the culture and history of their own world, and the entire structure of the novel seamless and unified.

SECONDARY SOURCES AND REVIEWS:

1. *Booklist* 85 (January 1, 1989): 730.
2. Brown, Cathy. "Talking About Books," in *East Anglian Times* (December 16, 1989): .
3. Gilbert, John. *Fear* (January, 1990): 72.
4. *Kirkus Reviews* 56 (December 15, 1988): 1781.
5. *Library Journal* 114 (February 15, 1989): 179.
6. *Locus* 22 (February, 1989): 17.
7. *Locus* 23 (November, 1989): 56.
8. *Publishers Weekly* 234 (December 2, 1988): 48.
9. Rutledge, Amelia A. *Science Fiction & Fantasy Book Review Annual 1990*, edited by Robert A. Collins and Robert Latham. New York, Westport, CT: Greenwood Press, 1991, cloth, p. 335.
10. *School Library Journal* 36 (January, 1990): 128.
11. Sefton, Laurie. "No Prisoners," in *OtherRealms* no. 24 (1989): 21.
12. Sutton, Don. "A Call from a Can of Worms," in *Liverpool Daily Post* (January 11, 1990): .
13. *Voice of Youth Advocates* 12 (August, 1989): 166.

A15. *Deryni Magic.* New York: A Del Rey Book, Ballantine Books, January 1991, 370 p., paper (ISBN 0-345-36117-2), $5.95.   LC 90-93285. Cover art by Michael Herring. [nonfiction]

This guide provides much background material on the Deryni world, focusing specifically on the magical elements that provide underpinning to the characters, the Deryni themselves, and their psychic abilities.

CONTENTS: Foreword; Introduction: Deryni Magic: A Few Definitions; I. The Deryni: Originals and Historical Background; II. Religious Framework I: Structure of the Church, Religious Orders, and the Sacraments of Baptism and Matrimony; III. Religious Framework II: Holy Orders, Confession, Extreme Unction, and Eucharist; IV. Telepathic Functions I: General Definitions, Ethics, Shields, Mind-Speech, Energy Augmention; V. Telepathic Functions II: Rapport; VI. Telepathic Functions III: Truth-Reading, Memory, Mind-Control, and Staring Patterns; VII. Clairsentient Functions; VIII. Telefunctions I: Telekinesis; IX. Telefunctions II: Transfer Portals; X. Operative Magic I: Utility Spells and the Duel Arcane; XI. Operative Magic II: Shape-Changing; XII. Wards and Warding: The Guardians of the Quarters; XIII. Ward Cubes I: Basics;

XIV. Ward Cubes II: Adavanced Permutations; XV. Healers and the Healing Function; XVI. The Training of Healers I; XVII. The Training of Healers II: "The *Examen*"; XVIII. Dark Magic; XIX. Were-Deryni: The Haldane Subset and Others Who Do Not Fit the Usual Definitions; XX. Ritual I: Definitions and Physical Setup; XXI. Ritual II: Casting the Circle and Warding the Working Place; XXII. Ritual III: Ending the Ritual and Summary; XXIII. Ritual IV: Applications.

Appendix I: Dioceses of Gwynedd and Surrounds; Appendix II: Various Bishops of Gwynedd; Appendix III: Religious Orders in Gwynedd; Appendix IV: Portal Locations in Gwynedd; Appendix V: The *Adsum Domine*: The Healer's Invocation; Appendix VI: Deryni Esoteric Terms; Appendix VII: Members of the Camberian Council Through 918; Appendix VIII: Glossary of Deryni Terms; Index of Magic; Partial Lineage of the Haldane Kings; The Festillic Kings of Gwynedd and Their Descendants; Partial Lineage of the MacRories.

Two original short stories are embedded in the text: "First Session" in Chapter XVI and "The *Examen*" as the entire Chapter XVII; in addition, many passages are quoted from the published novels and stories in the series to illustrate specific points (with exact citations). The Index of Magic is a useful subject guide to different occurrences of particular powers and forces (e.g., "Mind-Ripping," "*Shiral* Crystals," and "Attuning"). Although this is not a master index to the people and places of the Deryni otherworld, it nonetheless synthesizes so much background data into one manual that *Deryni Magic* will prove essential to anyone who is a devoted reader of the series.

SECONDARY SOURCES AND REVIEWS:

1. Cushman, Carolyn. *Locus* 26 (February, 1991): 27-28.
2. *Publishers Weekly* 237 (December 21, 1990): 50.
3. Sefton, Laurie. "No Prisoners." *OtherRealms* no. 28 (1991): 38.

A16. *The Adept*, by Katherine Kurtz and Deborah Turner Harris. The Adept, Volume 1. New York: Ace Books, March 1991, 321 p., paper (ISBN 0-441-00343-5), $4.95. Cover art by Tom Kidd. [supernatural novel]

b. New York: Ace Books, August 1992, 323 p., cloth (ISBN 0-7278-4378-8), $20.00. This is actually an importation of the Severn House edition.
c. Wallington, Surrey: Severn House, 1992, 323 p., cloth (ISBN 0-7278-4382-6). The jacket art, which is different from the Ace edition, is uncredited.
cb. Wallington, Surrey: Severn House, 1992, 323 p., trade paper (ISBN 0-7278-5031-8).

The first book in this new series introduces Sir Adam Sinclair, a Scottish psychiatrist who also belongs to a secret society of adepts and psychic police who track down practitioners of black magic, bring them to justice, and try to rectify the damage they've caused.

Adam takes under his wing Peregrine Lovat, a painter whose ability to "see" beyond the ordinary has pushed him to the brink of suicide. Adam shows Peregrine that his talents can be controlled and used for the benefit of mankind, and brings him into the case which is now developing.

An ancient sword has been stolen and a man murdered, a twelfth-century sorcerer's tomb disturbed and the corpse animated, and the Fairy Flag of the MacLeod clan taken from its display case (and the hired thief killed by her employers). Adam determines that a new group of magicians is trying to open a fairy cave in Scotland, and to steal the dead sorcerer's book of spells. Arriving just in the nick in time with Peregrine and Inspector McLeod (a relative of the MacLeod clan), Adam stops the desecration, watches as the despoilers are destroyed by the fairies, and placates the spirits into returning to their underground abode. An equilibrium has been restored, but the signs are plain: the Lodge of the Lynx, an ancient society of black magicians, has been revived!

Copyrighted with Bill Fawcett, who packaged and sold the series.

SECONDARY SOURCES AND REVIEWS:

1. *Library Journal* 116 (March 15, 1991): 119.
2. *Publishers Weekly* 238 (February 8, 1991): 54.
3. *School Library Journal* 37 (September, 1991): 298.

A17.   *The Lodge of the Lynx*, by Katherine Kurtz and Deborah Turner Harris. The Adept, Volume 2. New York: Ace Books, June 1992, 426 p., paper (ISBN 0-441-00344-3), $4.99. Cover art by Tom Kidd. [super-natural novel]

In this direct sequel to *The Adept*, psychiatrist and psychic detective Sir Adam Sinclair, Master of the Hunt, and his companions, Peregrine Lovat and Inspector McLeod, confront a baffling series of seemingly directed lightning strikes and attacks against freemasonry in Scotland and England, all linked to the rise of the Lodge of the Lynx.

After several dozen masons are murdered, some of them ritually, Adam and the Hunters track the Lodge to its lair in the highlands of Scotland. The Head-Master of darkness is revealed to be Rudolf Hess, Hitler's former deputy, who had smuggled the Führer's *Black Book* of spells out of Germany in 1941, was replaced with a double who impersonated him in prison, and who is now using black magic to assert his own power.

With the help of the spiritual forces of good, Adam and his companions rout Hess's minions, and the evil Master is himself carried off into the heavens. But Hess's chief lieutenant, Francis Raeburn, escapes to fight Sinclair another day.

The mention of Hitler's *Black Book* links this novel directly to Kurtz's earlier novel of occult warfare, *Lammas Night* (A7).

SECONDARY SOURCES AND REVIEWS:

1.   Cushman, Carolyn. *Locus* 29 (July, 1992): 33.

A18.   *King Javan's Year.* Volume II of The Heirs of Saint Camber. New York: A Del Rey Book, Ballantine Books, December 1992, xiii + 490 p., cloth (ISBN 0-345-33260-1), $20.00. LC 92-53218. Cover art by Michael Herring. [fantasy novel]

The persecution of the Deryni continues in the eleventh novel in the Cycle (the fifth of the sequence beginning with *Camber of Culdi*). In the year 921 young King Alroy is dying. His legal heir and twin, Prince Javan, rides from the abbey where he has been studying, and assumes the throne. The new king, although slightly handicapped physically, is a much brighter, stronger, and more capable ruler than his brother, and immediately sets out to establish his authority.

The former regents, however, continue their plotting behind his back. Archbishop Hubert schemes to have the king's younger brother, Rhys Michael, married to Michaela Drummond, for if either prince can be made to produce an heir, disposing of either or both adult Haldanes will become that much easier, with a long period of regencies to follow. With the help of Abbot Paulin, notorious head of the Deryni-hunting Ordo Custodem Fidei (popularly known as the Custodes) and his brother, Lord Albertus, Hubert has Rhys kidnapped, ostensibly by Deryni, and removes him to the friendly estate where Michaela resides. There the two lovers are married, and Michaela quickly becomes pregnant.

Two of Javan's enemies, Murdoch Earl of Carthane and Inquisitor General Brother Serafin, are eliminated by the king's friends, but the effort proves too little, too late. Javan and his men are ambushed and killed by Hubert and Paulin, who simultaneously stage a palace coup which places a compliant Rhys on the throne. A brief year of light is followed by re-establishment of the status quo.

Once again, Kurtz's characters are carefully drawn and memorable, the political and religious tensions of her world strictly rendered, and the settings as realistic as fantasy can be. One is struck, both in this novel and its predecessors, by the parallels between the intolerance, fear, and prejudice exhibited in these stories and in our own everyday world. We need only to look around us to see the same forces at work, with similarly violent consequences. Yet, for all the grimness these tales display, Kurtz is always careful to offer in them a glimmer of hope, a sense that only order, reason, faith, justice, and love can provide a counterbalance to hate and the chaos it engenders. Individual kings may die, she says, but the House of Haldane goes on, and will eventually triumph.

SECONDARY SOURCES AND REVIEWS:

1. Cushman, Carolyn. *Locus* 29 (November, 1992): 29.
2. Green, Roland. "Kurtz' New Deryni Novel Keeps Pace with Others."
   Chicago Sun-Times (December __, 1992): .

A19.   *The Templar Treasure*, by Katherine Kurtz and Deborah Turner Harris. The Adept, Volume 3. New York: Ace Books, June 1993, p., paper. Cover art by Tom Kidd. [supernatural novel]

After a burglary in which an old Jewish scholar is mortally injured and a mysterious seal is stolen—which may just be *the* Seal of Solomon—Adam and fellow huntsmen Noel McLeod and Peregrine Lovat go down to Kent to consult a very old John Graham, who knew Adam's mother during World War II. Graham is now the keeper of a Templar neck cross said to have been worn by John Graham of Claverhouse, "Bonnie Dundee," when he fell at the Battle of Killiecrankie.

Using the Templar cross to communicate directly with the spirit of Dundee, Graham assists in discovering what the stolen seal guards: not, as the thief believes, a casket of Solomonic treasures long protected by the Knights Templar, but the demons Gog and Magog, locked away by King Solomon himself.

Adam's mission: to find the thief and the seal before it's too late, and, if necessary, to put the genie back into the bottle—which also requires Solomon's crown and sceptre. Templar crypto-history continues to unfold as Adam and company take the chase first to Scotland's Fyvie Castle, then to Roslyn Chapel, and finally to what remains of the ancient Templar preceptory of Balantrodoch, just south of Edinburgh.

Drawing on his power and the authority of King Solomon himself, Adam orders the demons back into the casket, seals it underground for another few millennia, and deals with the now-mad thief, who will probably end up as a patient of his.

Brigadier John Graham, a major character in this new work, was also featured (as a much younger man) in *Lammas Night* (see A7), thereby cementing the links between the two series.

A20. *The Captive Kings.* Volume III of The Heirs of Saint Camber. New York: A Del Rey Book, Ballantine Books, 1993, p., cloth. [fantasy novel]

The final volume in the fourth trilogy will deal with the short and tragic reign of King Rhys Michael (922-928), and the threat of the Festillic pretender, Prince Mark (or Marek, as he is known in Torenth), bastard son of King Imre and his sister.

The book was originally announced as *The Bastard Prince*, "but the new title is a much better descriptor"—Katherine Kurtz. The manuscript was reported near completion at the end of 1992.

B.

SHORT FICTION

B1. "Swords Against the Marluk," in *Flashing Swords! #4: Barbarians and Black Magicians*, edited by Lin Carter. Garden City, NY: Nelson Doubleday, 1977, cloth, p. 107-134. This Book Club edition appeared before the paperback version.

    ab. *Flashing Swords! #4: Barbarians and Black Magicians*, edited by Lin Carter. New York: A Dell Book, November 1977, paper, p. 161-201.

    b. as: "Des Marluks Untergang," in *Ashtaru der Schreckliche*, edited by Erhard Ringer and Hermann Urbanek. München: Wilhelm Heyne Verlag, 1982, paper, p. 143-180. [German]

    c. *Barbarians*, edited by Robert Adams, Martin H. Greenberg, and Charles G. Waugh. New York: New American Library, January 1986, paper, p. 217-241.

    cb. as: "Marluk," in *Barbarzyncy*, edited by Robert Adams, Martin H. Greenberg, and Charles G. Waugh. Poznan: Publishing House REBIS Ltd., 1991, paper, p. 143-175. [Polish]

Set in the year 1105, Kurtz's first published short fiction deals with Kelson's father, King Brion, and Brion's assumption of magical powers when faced with the threat of Hogan Gwernach (the "Marluk"), Festillic pretender to the throne of Gwynedd and father of Kelson's rival, Charissa. Nothing has been heard of the Festils or their claims for generations, and apparently none of the Haldane kings has been called to his heritage during the previous century. However, the old King, Donal Blaine, had implanted the activation ritual in the mind of four-year-old Alaric Morgan some ten years earlier. Alaric, now Brion's squire, initiates the ritual when Brion receives the written challenge from Hogan. Brion then confronts the usurper, and defeats him in a duel arcane. Hogan's daughter Charissa escapes, later to avenge her father and murder Brion, and then challenge his son, King Kelson.

    Much of this story will be incorporated into the projected trilogy dealing with the early life of Alaric Morgan, Duke of Corwyn, and King Brion Haldane.

B2.   "Lords of Sorandor," in *The Deryni Archives* no. 1 (December, 1978): 16-31; and no. 2 (July, 1979): 18-30.

   b.   *The Deryni Archives*, by Katherine Kurtz. New York: A Del Rey Book, Ballantine Books, August 1986, paper, p. 256-303.

The first attempt at a Deryni story was written in October, 1965, a year after Kurtz had her original dream. In this version, Gwynedd is Sorandor, and Kelson's mother is Sanil rather than Jehana. However, many of the other key characters, including Morgan and Duncan, appear in recognizable form, with personae very similar to what they would become in the novels. The Deryni are not mentioned.

   The story line of this novella basically follows that of two key sections of *Deryni Rising*, dealing with Kelson's assumption of magical powers, and his duel of witchcraft with the "Blue One" (later Charissa).

B3.   "Healer's Song," in *Darkover Grand Council Meeting III* (Program Book), 1980, paper, p. 4-7.

   b.   *Fantasy Book* 1 (August, 1982): 54-59.
   c.   as: "Healer's Song: August 1, 914," in *The Deryni Archives*, by Katherine Kurtz. New York: A Del Rey Book, Ballantine Books, August 1986, paper, p. 28-44.

The convention was held November 28-30, 1980, at the Radisson Hotel, Wilmington, DE.

   This very short story deals with one incident in the year 914, during the birth of Tieg, healer son of Evaine MacRorie (daughter of Camber of Culdi) and the healer Deryni, Rhys Thuryn.

B4.   "Legacy," in *Darkover Grand Council IV* (Program Book), 1981, paper, p. 23-28.

   b.   *Fantasy Book* 2 (February, 1983): 50-54.
   c.   as: "Legacy: June 21, 1105," in *The Deryni Archives*, by Katherine Kurtz. New York: A Del Rey Book, Ballantine Books, August 1986, paper, p. 158-172.

The convention was held November 27-29, 1981, at the Radisson Hotel, Wilmington, DE.

   Set in the summer of 1105, Kurtz's short story tells of the confrontation between King Brion, Kelson's father, and Hogan Gwernach, Festillic claimant to the throne of Gwynedd, and father of Charissa (who was later to kill Brion and then herself die in a contest of magic with King Kelson). Told from the viewpoint of Charissa and her cousins, the royal princes and kings of Torenth, "Legacy" provides significant insights into the future of Prince Wencit, who at this stage of his career is a seemingly distant third in line to the throne of Torenth; and also demonstrates the legacy of hate which has permeated relations between humans and the Deryni over the preceding three centuries.

B5.   "Camber the Heretic," in *Fantasy Book* 1 (December, 1981): 16-27.

The first chapter of the novel of the same name (see A6).

B6.   "Bethane," in *Hecate's Cauldron*, edited by Susan Shwartz. New York: DAW Books, 1982, paper, p. 190-206.

   b.   as: "Bethane: Summer, 1100," in *The Deryni Archives*, by Katherine Kurtz. New York: A Del Rey Book, Ballantine Books, August 1986, paper, p. 77-98.

This interesting tale takes a minor character from *Deryni Checkmate*, Bethane, the almost stereotypical hag of the hills, and examines her life twenty years earlier, in the Summer of the year 1100. Young Alaric Morgan takes a spill from a tree, and Bethane must choose to harm—or help— the young Deryni lad. In the process she remembers how her Deryni husband had been murdered by a mob years before, starting her on the path to a bitter and lonely old age. She redeems herself partially by helping set the boy's arm.

B7.   "Vocation," in *Nine Visions: A Book of Fantasies*, edited by Andrea La-Sonde Melrose. New York: Seabury Press, 1983, paper, p. 109-133.

   b.   as: "Vocation: December 24, 977," in *The Deryni Archives*, by Katherine Kurtz. New York: A Del Rey Book, Ballantine Books, August 1986, paper, p. 45-76.

Near the end of the year 977, at the height of the state-sponsored persecution against the Deryni, a young knight, Gilrae d'Eirial, must choose between his imminent succession to the barony of that name and his vocation to become a priest. He is aided in his decision by an old Deryni healer, Simonn, who cures him of the cancer in his arm, and thus gives him the opportunity to renounce his worldly title in favor of his half-brother, Caprus.

     For the prequel, in which Simonn is shown being trained sixty years earlier, see "First Session" (B16).

B8. "Catalyst," in *Moonsinger's Friends: An Anthology in Honor of Andre Norton*, edited by Susan Shwartz. New York: Bluejay Books, June 1985, cloth, p. 314-326. Published simultaneously in trade paperback.

   ab. *Moonsinger's Friends: An Anthology in Honor of Andre Norton*, edited by Susan Shwartz. New York: Tor SF, A Tom Doherty Associates Book, 1986, paper, p. 314-326.

   ac. *Moonsinger's Friends: An Anthology in Honor of Andre Norton*, edited by Susan Shwartz. London: Severn House, 1986, cloth, p. 314-326.

   b. as: "Catalyst: Fall, 888," in *The Deryni Archives*, by Katherine Kurtz. New York: A Del Rey Book, Ballantine Books, August 1986, paper, p. 10-27.

The earliest Deryni story yet written, "Catalyst" is set in Fall of 888, fifteen years before the opening scenes of *Camber of Culdi*. Rhys Thuryn, an orphan lad who has been raised by Earl Camber MacRorie and his family (and the future husband of Camber's daughter, Evaine) discovers his healing abilities when he and his pet cat are injured during a brush with robbers.

B9. "The Priesting of Arilan: August 1, 1104-February 2, 1105," in *The Deryni Archives*, by Katherine Kurtz. New York: A Del Rey Book, Ballantine Books, August 1986, paper, p. 99-157.

One of the truly horrific strictures of the councils of state and church which assumed power in Gwynedd in 917 was a promulgation forbidding any Deryni from becoming a priest. The Deryni were assumed to be evil *per se*, and were thus barred on the pain of death from being ordained. Those who tried were all discovered and executed, usually being burned at the stake as heretics. Kurtz's story, set in the years 1104-1105, deals with the first successful ordination of a Deryni priest, in the person of Denis Arilan, who was later to become a bishop and play a key role in the revolution which gradually restored the Deryni race to a level of respectability. This poignant tale demonstrates the depth of Arilan's faith in a merciful God, a belief which sustains him and his kind even in the depths of despair. Arilan's ordination will provide the opportunity for the creation of other Deryni priests.

B10. "The Knighting of Derry: May, 1115," in *The Deryni Archives*, by Katherine Kurtz. New York: A Del Rey Book, Ballantine Books, August 1986, paper, p. 173-204.

Sean Lord Derry, Duke Alaric Morgan's aide in the Kelson novels, is a curious figure, seemingly content to play second fiddle to the more glamorous Morgan. Set five years before the events in *Deryni Rising*,

"Knighting" shows us how the relationships of the key men supporting Kelson's shaky throne were beginning to come together, even before King Brion's untimely death, and how their common ideals would eventually be translated into the final ending of the Deryni persecutions.

B11.   "Trial: Spring, 1118," in *The Deryni Archives*, by Katherine Kurtz. New York: A Del Rey Book, Ballantine Books, August 1986, paper, p. 205-230.

In many respects "Trial" is somewhat peripheral to the Deryni saga, having been generated by an auction at a science-fiction convention in which the grand prize for the winners was realization as characters in a page or two of a new Katherine Kurtz story. Ferris, a foreign sword-maker, is assaulted by tavern patrons and accused of murder. At his trial he appears well on the way to the gallows when Duke Alaric Morgan (whose land this is) intervenes, determines the truth of the matter, and points out the real murderers. In gratitude, Ferris offers to make the Duke a "real" sword, and to enter his service in the future.

B12.   "The Dream That Became Deryni," in *The Deryni Archives*, by Katherine Kurtz. New York: A Del Rey Book, Ballantine Books, August 1986, paper, p. 255.

A transcription of the vivid dream experienced by the author on 11 October 1964, a summary of which was immediately jotted down on two 3" x 5" cards. This marks the inception of the entire Deryni series.

B13.   "Precis of *Deryni Rising*," in *The Deryni Archives*, by Kathérine Kurtz. New York: A Del Rey Book, Ballantine Books, August 1986, paper, p. 304-305.

A two-page plot summary of the first Deryni trilogy, part of a book prospectus submitted to Ballantine Books in 1969.

B14.   "Submission Outline for *Deryni Rising*," in *The Deryni Archives*, by Katherine Kurtz. New York: A Del Rey Book, Ballantine Books, August 1986, paper, p. 306-325.

As part of the original proposal made by Kurtz to Ballantine Books in 1969 (see B12), the author prepared a detailed plot summary, chapter by chapter, of the first book in the sequence, which in turn had been expanded from the original novella, "Lords of Sorandor" (see B2).

B15. "Manstopper," by Katherine Kurtz and Scott MacMillan, in *Total War: The Fleet, Book 5*, edited by David Drake and Bill Fawcett. New York: Ace Books, September 1990, paper, p. 215-241.

David Drake and Bill Fawcett have created a proprietary science fiction universe in which the Human/Alien Alliance (The Fleet) battles invaders from Khalia, defeats them, and then joins with them to fight the Syndicate of Families in an ongoing struggle for the control of known space. Each of the six books in the series features contributions by a dozen authors, with bridge passages by the editors.

"Manstopper" centers on Rykker, a spy for The Fleet, who must fight for his life on a hot desert planet. Using the technology left in an abandoned mine, he constructs a replica of a Colt six-shooter, and uses the weapon to overcome his adversaries. This is Kurtz's first SF short story, and the first written in collaboration with her husband, whose knowledge of modern weaponry and personal survival tactics is very evident here. Kurtz's contributions consist mainly of editorial polishing.

B16. "First Session," in *Deryni Magic*, by Katherine Kurtz. New York: A Del Rey Book, Ballantine Books, January 1991, paper, p. 202-210.

"First Session" expands upon an incident recorded in *Camber the Heretic* (p. 174-175 of the Ballantine paperback edition), in which Camber visits Saint Neot's Abbey in the year 917, and there witnesses a Deryni healer novice (Simonn de Beaumont) being trained by Dom Kilian. The brief passage quoted from *Heretic* falls midway through the story, which Kurtz has built into a vignette designed to demonstrate how healing skills were nurtured and bolstered.

For a similar sequence, see "The *Examen*" (B17); and for the sequel, in which Simonn heals a baron's arm, see "Vocation" (B7).

B17. "The *Examen*," in *Deryni Magic*, by Katherine Kurtz. New York: A Del Rey Book, Ballantine Books, January 1991, paper, p. 213-224.

This original short story provides further details of Deryni healer training. Since corpses of outsiders were unavailable for dissection and training, due to cultural taboos, each of the brothers resident in the monastery willed his body to the community for dissection on the day after his death. Here Dom Kilian MacShane, the brother who is seen training Simonn in "First Session," is himself undergoing training as a novice earlier in his life (circa 905). He assists at the dissection of a fellow novice who had gone mad the day before, killed one of the masters, and was himself shot down before he could cause any further damage. The mixture of loss, duty, and devotion leaves a lasting impression on the reader.

B18. "Distress Signals," by Scott MacMillan and Katherine Kurtz, in *Crisis: The Fleet, Book 6*, edited by David Drake and Bill Fawcett. New York: Ace Books, February 1991, paper, p. 146-171.

In Kurtz and MacMillan's second contribution to this series (see also B15 above), Commander Talley, a former battlecruiser commander, is reassigned to an old supply ship whose main computer uses an experimental hydroponic plant system to help run the vessel.

When the cargo ship is attacked by a Syndicate raider, and most of his crew precipitously abandon ship, Talley and his handful of officers must use his battle experience and the unique (plant) resources at hand to defeat the boarders.

Kurtz's contributions consist mainly of editorial polishing.

B19. "The Tinkling of Fairybells," in *Once Upon a Time: A Treasury of Modern Fairy Tales*, edited by Lester del Rey and Rita Kessler. New York: A Del Rey Book, Ballantine Books, November 1991, cloth, p. 227-245. Includes a color plate by Michael Pangrazio illustrating the story.

ab. *Once Upon a Time: A Treasury of Modern Fairy Tales*, edited by Lester del Rey and Rita Kessler. New York: A Del Rey Book, Ballantine Books, November 1991, trade paper, p. 227-245. Includes a color plate by Michael Pangrazio illustrating the story.

ac. *Once Upon a Time: A Treasury of Modern Fairy Tales*, edited by Lester del Rey and Rita Kessler. London: Legend, November 1991, cloth, p. 227-245.

A fairy witnesses what she considers to be a magical ceremony conducted at a forest chapel by an altar boy who later becomes Father Peter. Over the years the two beings, one spirit, one flesh, gradually attain almost a symbiotic relationship of love and respect through the continuing mystery of the mass. Eventually Father Peter dies in a shipwreck while the fairy helplessly sees him perish, unable to assist her companion of the real world. She stands watch over his tomb, and is rewarded when the soul of the priest returns, and the two spirits are reunited in an ecstasy of eternal glory.

This short tale represents perhaps the purest expression to date of Kurtz's belief in a universe where the physical and spiritual not only coexist, but overlap at almost every level. If we but open our eyes, we will see and experience wonders beyond our imagining.

B20. "The Summoning: Anno Domini 1773," in *The Crafters*, edited by Christopher Stasheff and Bill Fawcett. New York: Ace Books, December 1991, paper, p. 210-223.

This anthology of stories is set against the background of a fictional family, the Crafters, who have passed various magical talents to their offspring over a ten-generation span, from the late sixteen hundreds to the present day; and who use their powers to benefit mankind, by providing guidance to specific individuals destined to have a major impact on human history.

In "The Summoning," Jakob Crafter and his two children use magic to draw a tall stranger (George Washington) to their wilderness home, and tell him that he is destined to lead his country to freedom as their anointed savior.

B21.   "Sir James the Rose," by Scott MacMillan and Katherine Kurtz, in *The Gods of War*, edited by Christopher Stasheff and Bill Fawcett. Riverdale, NY: Baen Books, December 1992, paper, p. .

B22.   "Battle Offering," by Scott MacMillan and Katherine Kurtz, in as yet an untitled Battle Station anthology, edited by Christopher Stasheff and Bill Fawcett. Riverdale, NY: Baen Books, 1993, paper, p. .

C.

SHORT NONFICTION

C1.   "The Historian As Myth-Maker and Vice Versa," in *Fantasiae* 1 (August, 1973): 1-3. [literature]

b.   *Bulletin of the Science Fiction Writers of America* 13 (Fall, 1978): 16-18.

C2.   "About Our Cover: A Crash Course on Deryni Heraldry," by "B. Fraser," in *Deryni Archives* no. 1 (December, 1978): 7. [heraldry]

C3.   "Update on the Naming of Morgan," in *Deryni Archives* no. 1 (December, 1978): 14. [report]

C4.   "In the Beginning: The Birth of the Deryni Series," in *Deryni Archives* no. 1 (December, 1978): 15. [Deryni]

C5.   "A Marion Zimmer Bradley Appreciation," in *Darkover Grand Council Meeting II*, 1979, paper, p. 5-7. [appreciation]

C6.   "Status Report," in *Deryni Archives* no. 2 (July, 1979): 1-2. [progress report]

C7.   "Our Cover Heraldry," by "B. Fraser," in *Deryni Archives* no. 2 (July, 1979): 3-7. [heraldry]

C8.   "Status Report from Katherine Kurtz," in *Deryni Archives* no. 3 (October, 1979): 2. [progress report]

C9.   "On the Heraldry and Habiliments of the Order of St. Michael: A Precis," by Katherine Kurtz and Michael C. Mahaney, in *Deryni Archives* no. 3 (October, 1979): 3. [heraldry]

C10.   "We Get Letters, with Answers from Katherine Kurtz," in *Deryni Archives* no. 3 (October, 1979): 8-11. [Deryni]

C11.   "From Camber's Library: Suggested Background Reading," non-by-lined, in *Deryni Archives* no. 3 (October, 1979): 16. [reviews]

C12. "The Heraldic Field, Ordinaries, and Sub-Ordinaries," by "B. Fraser," in *Deryni Archives* no. 3 (October, 1979): 17-20. [heraldry]

C13. "In the Beginning: The Birth of the Deryni Series, Part III," in *Deryni Archives* no. 3 (October, 1979): 22-34. [Deryni]

C14. "Progress Report from Katherine Kurtz," in *Deryni Archives* no. 4 (May, 1980): 2. [progress report]

C15. "Basic Blazoning," by "B. Fraser," in *Deryni Archives* no. 4 (May, 1980): 4-6. [heraldry]

C16. "From Camber's Library," in *Deryni Archives* no. 4 (May, 1980): 34. [reviews]

C17. "Imaginary History: A Genealogical Approach," in *Chicago Fantasy Newsletter* 2 (June/July, 1980): 6-9. [literature]

b. *The Work of Katherine Kurtz: An Annotated Bibliography & Guide*, by Boden Clarke with Mary A. Burgess. San Bernardino, CA: The Borgo Press, 1993, cloth, p. 117-123. Published simultaneously in trade paper.

C18. "Progress Report from Katherine Kurtz," in *Deryni Archives* no. 5 (October, 1980): 2-4. [progress report]

C19. "Cadency," by "B. Fraser," in *Deryni Archives* no. 5 (October, 1980): 26-29. [heraldry]

C20. "From Camber's Library," in *Deryni Archives* no. 5 (October, 1980): 30. [reviews]

C21. "Progress Report from Katherine Kurtz," in *Deryni Archives* no. 6 (February, 1981): 2-3. [progress report]

C22. "From Camber's Library," non-bylined, in *Deryni Archives* no. 6 (February, 1981): 11-12. [reviews]

C23. "A Liturgical Calendar," non-bylined, in *Deryni Archives* no. 6 (February, 1981): 27-28. [religion]

C24. "Marshalling Arms," by "B. Fraser," in *Deryni Archives* no. 6 (February, 1981): 29-31. [heraldry]

C25. "Progress Report from Katherine Kurtz," in *Deryni Archives* no. 7 (October, 1981): 2-3. [progress report]

C26.   **"Heraldic Badges,"** by "B. Fraser," in *Deryni Archives* no. 7 (October, 1981): 14-15. [heraldry]

C27.   **"From Camber's Library,"** non-bylined, in *Deryni Archives* no. 7 (October, 1981): 33. [reviews]

C28.   **"Progress Report from Katherine Kurtz,"** in *Deryni Archives* no. 8 (June, 1982): 2. [progress report]

C29.   **"Titles and Forms of Address in Gwynedd,"** by "B. Fraser," in *Deryni Archives* no. 8 (June, 1982): 23. [Deryni]

C30.   **"Progress Report from Katherine Kurtz,"** in *Deryni Archives* no. 9 (February, 1983): 2-3. [progress report]

C31.   **"Vestments and Other Accoutrements,"** by "B. Fraser," in *Deryni Archives* no. 9 (February, 1983): 14-18. [religion]

C32.   **"From Camber's Library,"** non-bylined, in *Deryni Archives* no. 9 (February, 1983): 35. [reviews]

C33.   **"Progress Report from Katherine Kurtz,"** in *Deryni Archives* no. 10 (March, 1984): 2-4. [progress report]

C34.   **"Church Architecture,"** by "B. Fraser," in *Deryni Archives* no. 10 (March, 1984): 17-19. [religion]

C35.   **"Progress Report,"** in *Deryni Archives* no. 11 (Spring 1985): 2. [progress report]

C36.   **"Holy Orders: A Brief Overview,"** in *Deryni Archives* no. 11 (Spring 1985): 18-20. [religion]

C37.   **"Introduction,"** in *The Deryni Archives*, by Katherine Kurtz. New York: A Del Rey Book, Ballantine Books, August 1986, paper, p. 1-9. Kurtz also contributed new headnotes for each story. [introduction]

C38.   **"Introduction,"** in *Deryni Challenge*, by Stephen Billias. New York: A Crossroads Adventure, Tor, A Tom Doherty Associates Book, April 1988, paper, p. 1-5. [introduction]

D.

SONGS

D1. "Gwydion's Song," in *Deryni Archives* no. 2 (July, 1979): 31.

D2. "Fair Fallen Lord," in *Deryni Archives* no. 5 (October, 1980): 4.

D3. "Adsum, Domine," in *Deryni Archives* no. 7 (October, 1981): 16. In Latin.

D4. "The Healers' Hymn," in *Deryni Archives* no. 7 (October, 1981): 17. An English-language version of D3.

D5. "Fal Morgan," sung by Jim Fox-Davis with Catherine Cook as instrumentalist, on *Songs of the Dorsai!* El Cerrito, CA: Off Centaur Publishing, 1983, cassette tape.

E.

EDITORIAL CREDITS

E1.   *The Deryni Archives.* Katherine Kurtz, Publisher and Editor. Sun Valley,
       CA: Caer Deryni Publications, nos. 1-10, 1978-1984.

A magazine published for Katherine Kurtz fans, including news of Kurtz's
new works, stories, background material on the Deryni world, articles on
heraldry, etc. Joyce Muskat served as Editor of the first issue. The publication was given to Mary Greeley and Yvonne John in 1985.

a.   No. 1, December, 1978 (reprinted July, 1981)
b.   No. 2, July, 1979 (reprinted January, 1984)
c.   No. 3, October, 1979 (reprinted September, 1985)
d.   No. 4, May, 1980 (reprinted September, 1985)
e.   No. 5, October, 1980
f.   No. 6, February, 1981
g.   No. 7, October, 1981
h.   No. 8, June, 1982
i.   No. 9, February, 1983
j.   No. 10, March, 1984

The Greeley/John Issues:

aa.   No. 11, Spring, 1985
ab.   No. 12, Fall 1986
ac.   No. 13, Spring 1989
ad.   No. 14, 1992

F.

SCRIPTS

F1.   Kurtz developed three scripts circa 1975 for the very first scenarios used by the Los Angeles Police Department for its shooting simulator, to train police officers to respond to crisis situations where they may or may not be confronted by a gunman.

G.

OTHER MEDIA

G1.   *An Hour with Marion Zimmer Bradley: A Personal Note*, interviewed by
      Katherine Kurtz.   Bob and Mary Drayer, Editors; Marion Zimmer
      Bradley and Mary Drayer, Writers; Mike Lefebvre, Creative Consultant.
      Garden Grove, CA: Hourglass Productions, 1978, 60-minute cassette
      tape. [audio cassette recording]

G2.   "The Deryni: An Adaptation," by Arthur Collins, in *Dragon* 8 (October,
      1983): 34-40. A Dungeons and Dragons role-model game, with rules,
      description, and specifications. [game]

G3.   *Deryni Challenge: A Crossroads Adventure in the World of Katherine
      Kurtz's Deryni*, by Stephen Billias. New York: Tor SF, A Tom Doherty
      Associates Book, April 1988, 27 + [222] p., paper.   [interactive game
      book].

      In the year 905, the Deryni nobleman Geordie Drummond, son of Henry
      Drummond, nephew of Jamie Drummond, and cousin to Camber of Culdi,
      is involved in a series of adventures a few months after the restoration of
      the Haldane line and the deposition and death of the Deryni King Imre.
      Through a series of individual choices and rolls of the dice, the reader can
      take Geordie through a series 101 different story lines involving magic, ad-
      venture, and the use of mental powers. Kurtz contributes a five-page in-
      troduction outlining the historical background of the period and character.

H.

UNPUBLISHED WORKS

H1.   "The Naming of Morgan." A short story which will be developed into the Childe Morgan trilogy.

H2.   *The Legacy of Lehr.* A novel sold to Laser Books circa 1975, but never published by them. It was extensively rewritten for publication by Walker & Co. in 1986 (see A13).

H3.   *Deryni Rising: A Screenplay*, by Don Marrs and Katherine Kurtz. 138 manuscript pages, about 1977.

H4.   Approximately 150 pages were cut by Kurtz from her novel, *Camber the Heretic*, prior to its publication in 1981 (see also A6), much of it later incorporated into *The Harrowing of Gwynedd*.

H5.   A manuscript binder containing detailed genealogies of the chief families in the Deryni universe. This and Kurtz's other master notebooks are updated constantly as new books and stories in the series are being written.

H6.   A manuscript binder containing detailed chronologies of the major events in the Deryni timeline.

H7.   A manuscript binder containing detailed lists of characters from the Deryni universe, arranged by family.

H8.   A manuscript binder with songs, poems, and other miscellanea relating to the Deryni world.

I.

HONORS AND AWARDS

I1.   **Edmond Hamilton Memorial Award**, 1977, for *Camber of Culdi*.

I2.   **Gandalf Award Nomination**, for Best Book-Length Fantasy, 1978, for *Saint Camber*.

I3.   **Balrog Award**, Best Novel, 1981 (1982), for *Camber the Heretic*.

I4.   *The Legacy of Lehr* received a citation in *Best Science Fiction Titles of 1986* from VOYA (Voice of Youth Advocates).

J.

SECONDARY SOURCES

J1.   "Kurtz, Katherine, 1944-   ," in *Contemporary Authors: A Bio-Biblio-graphical Guide to Current Authors and Their Works, Volumes 29-32*, edited by Ann Evory.   Detroit: Gale Research Co., 1972, cloth, p.   .   [bio-bibliography]

J2.   "Kurtz, Katherine," in *The Writers Directory, 1976-78*.   New York: St. Martin's Press, 1976, cloth, p.   .   [bio-bibliography]

J3.   "Katherine Kurtz (b. Coral Gables, Fla., 18 October 1944)," in *Who's Who in Horror and Fantasy Fiction*, by Mike Ashley.   London: Elm Tree Books, 1977, cloth, p. 109. [biography]

   ab.   New York: Taplinger Publishing Co., 1978, cloth, p. 109.   Published simultaneously in trade paperback.

J4.   *Modern Fantasy Revisited: Katherine Kurtz and a New Dimension for the Genre*, by Linda Richardson.   Cookeville, TN: Tennessee Technological University, 1977, 111 leaves, paper.   [master's thesis]

J5.   "Kurtz, Katherine, 1944-   ," in *Contemporary Authors: A Bio-Biblio-graphical Guide to Current Authors and Their Works, Volumes 29-32, First Revision*, edited by Ann Evory.   Detroit: Gale Research Co., 1978, cloth, p. 375.   [bio-bibliography]

J6.   "Kurtz, Katherine," in *The Writers Directory, 1980-82*.   New York: St. Martin's Press, 1979, cloth, p.   .   [bio-bibliography]

J7.   *An Hour with Katherine Kurtz: An Introduction to the Author and Her Work*, interviewed by Mary Drayer.   Bob and Mary Drayer, Editors; Mike Lefebvre, Creative Consultant; Bjo Trimble, Writing; Pat Ortega, Graphics; Tom Grant, Technical Assistance.   Garden Grove, CA: Hourglass Productions, 1978, 60-minute cassette tape.   [interview]

J. Secondary Sources

J8. "Kurtz, Katherine, 1944- ," in *The Hills of Faraway: A Guide to Fantasy*, by Diana Waggoner. New York: Atheneum, 1978, cloth, p. 213. [critique]

J9. "Katherine Kurtz," in *The Literature of Fantasy: A Comprehensive, Annotated Bibliography of Modern Fantasy Fiction*, by Roger C. Schlobin. New York & London: Garland Publishing, 1979, cloth, p. 137-138. [bibliography and critique]

J10. "Katherine Kurtz," in *Science Fiction and Fantasy Literature, a Checklist, 1700-1974; with, Contemporary Science Fiction Authors II*, by R. Reginald. Detroit: Gale Research Co., 1979, cloth, Vol. 1 (p. 301), Vol. 2 (p. 966). [bio-bibliography]

J11. "Kurtz, Katherine. *Deryni Rising*," in *Fantasy Literature: A Core Collection and Reference Guide*, by Marshall B. Tymn, Kenneth J. Zahorski, and Robert H. Boyer. New York & London: R. R. Bowker Co., 1979, cloth, p. 101. [critique]

J12. "Kurtz, Katherine. *Deryni Checkmate*," in *Fantasy Literature: A Core Collection and Reference Guide*, by Marshall B. Tymn, Kenneth J. Zahorski, and Robert H. Boyer. New York & London: R. R. Bowker Co., 1979, cloth, p. 101-102. [critique]

J13. "Kurtz, Katherine. *High Deryni*," in *Fantasy Literature: A Core Collection and Reference Guide*, by Marshall B. Tymn, Kenneth J. Zahorski, and Robert H. Boyer. New York & London: R. R. Bowker Co., 1979, cloth, p. 102-103. [critique]

J14. "Kurtz, Katherine. *Camber of Culdi*," in *Fantasy Literature: A Core Collection and Reference Guide*, by Marshall B. Tymn, Kenneth J. Zahorski, and Robert H. Boyer. New York & London: R. R. Bowker Co., 1979, cloth, p. 103. [critique]

J15. "Kurtz, Katherine. *Saint Camber*," in *Fantasy Literature: A Core Collection and Reference Guide*, by Marshall B. Tymn, Kenneth J. Zahorski, and Robert H. Boyer. New York & London: R. R. Bowker Co., 1979, cloth, p. 104. [critique]

J16. "Kurtz, Katherine (1944-)," in *The Science Fiction Encyclopedia*, edited by Peter Nicholls and John Clute. Garden City, NY: Doubleday & Co., 1979, cloth, p. 338. [critique]

   ab. *The Encyclopedia of Science Fiction*. London: Granada, 1979, cloth, p. 338. Published in trade paperback in 1981.

J17.   "Kurtz, Katherine," in *Lexikon der Science Fiction: Literatur 1*, edited by Hans-Joachim Alpers *et al*. München: Wilhelm Heyne Verlag, 1980, paper, p. 411-412. [bio-bibliography]

J18.   "Interview: Katherine Kurtz," conducted by Jeffrey M. Elliot, in *Fantasy Newsletter* no. 24 (May, 1980): 16-21; and no. 25 (June, 1980): 12-17, 31. [interview]

The most extensive interview with Kurtz published to date, based on written questions posed by Elliot. The lengthy written responses, touching on every aspect of Kurtz's life and work, are solely her contribution. See also the revised and expanded version (J46).

b.   as: "Katherine Kurtz: Tapestries of Medieval Wonder," in *Fantasy Voices: Interviews with American Fantasy Writers*, by Jeffrey M. Elliot. San Bernardino, CA: The Borgo Press, January 1982, cloth, p. 44-64. Published simultaneously in trade paperback. Includes a photo of Kurtz.

c.   as: "Katherine Kurtz: Interview Essay," in *Fantasists on Fantasy: A Collection of Critical Reflections*, edited by Robert H. Boyer and Kenneth J. Zahorski. New York: A Discus Book, Avon Books, February 1984, paper, p. 231-260.

J19.   "Bibliography: Katherine Kurtz," in *Darkover Grand Council IV*, November 27-29, 1981. Wilmington, DE: Darkover Grand Council IV, 1981, paper, p. 29. [bibliography]

J20.   "Kurtz, Katherine," in *The Writers Directory, 1982-84*. Detroit: Gale Research Co., 1981, cloth, p. . [bio-bibliography]

J21.   "Katherine Kurtz," in *A Reader's Guide to Fantasy*, edited by Baird Searles, Beth Meacham, and Michael Franklin. New York: Avon, July 1982, paper, p. 87-88. [critique]

J22.   "Katherine Kurtz," in *1983 Paperbacks for Junior-Senior High Classrooms & Libraries*. New York: Ballantine/Vintage Books, 1983, paper, p. 7, 10.

J23.   "Kurtz, Katherine," in *The Writers Directory, 1984-86*. Chicago: St. James Press, 1983, cloth, p. 560. [bio-bibliography]

J24.   "*The Deryni Trilogy*," by Brian Stableford, in *Survey of Modern Fantasy Literature*, edited by Frank N. Magill. Englewood Cliffs, NJ: Salem Press, 1983, cloth, Vol. 1, p. 360-365. [critique]

J25. "Katherine Kurtz: Her Life, Her Universe, and Everything," by George Laskowski, in *Lan's Lantern* no. 13 (August, 1983): 24-31. [profile]

J26. "Kurtz, Katherine," in *Who's Who in America, 43rd Edition, 1984-1985.* Chicago: Marquis Who's Who, 1984, cloth, v. 1, p. . [bio-bibliography]

J27. "Kurtz, Katherine (1944)," in *The Science Fiction Source Book,* edited by David Wingrove. Harlow, England: Longman, 1984, cloth, p. 181. [critique]

   ab. New York: Van Nostrand Reinhold Co., 1984, cloth, p. 181.

J28. "Kurtz, Katherine," in *The Writers Directory, 1986-88.* Chicago and London: St. James Press, 1986, cloth, p. 545. [bio-bibliography]

J29. "Katherine Kurtz," in *Merlin's Daughters: Contemporary Women Writers of Fantasy,* by Charlotte Spivack. Westport, CT & London: Greenwood Press, 1987, cloth, p. 87-99. [critique]

J30. "Kurtz, Katherine. *Lammas Night,*" in *Supernatural Fiction for Teens: 500 Good Paperbacks to Read for Wonderment, Fear, and Fun,* by Cosette Kies. Littleton, CO: Libraries Unlimited, 1987, paper, p. 44. [critique]

J31. "Katherine Kurtz: A Special Section for Katherine—Guest of Honor at Confusion 1987," by George "Lan" Laskowski, in *Lan's Lantern* no. 22 (February, 1987): 76-79. Includes reviews by Kathleen Coñat of *Camber of Culdi* and *Saint Camber,* and by Terry O'Brien of *The Quest for Saint Camber, The Deryni Archives,* and *The Legacy of Lehr.* [profile and critiques]

J32. "Kurtz, Katherine," in *The Writers Directory, 1988-90, Eighth Edition.* Chicago and London: St. James Press, 1988, cloth, p. 548. [bio-bibliography]

J33. "Kurtz, Katherine [Irene] (1944-)," in *The New Encyclopedia of Science Fiction,* edited by James Gunn. New York: Viking, 1988, cloth, p. 260-261. [critique]

J34. "Kurtz, Katherine Irene," in *The International Authors and Writers Who's Who, Eleventh Edition,* ed. by Ernest Kay. Cambridge, England: International Biographical Centre, 1989, cloth, p. 492. [bio-bibliography]

J35.   "Kurtz, Katherine," in *Contemporary Authors, New Revision Series, Volume 25: A Bio-Bibliographical Guide to Current Writers in Fiction, General Nonfiction, Poetry, Journalism, Drama, Motion Pictures, Television, and Other Fields*, edited by Hal May and Deborah A. Straub. Detroit: Gale Research Inc., 1989, cloth, p. 257. [bio-bibliography]

J36.   "Kurtz, Katherine," in *The Writers Directory, 1990-92, Ninth Edition.* Chicago and London: St. James Press, 1990, cloth, p. 574. [bio-bibliography]

J37.   "Kurtz, Katherine. Third Order of St. Michael," in *Independent Bishops: An International Directory*, edited by Gary L. Ward, Bertil Persson, Alan Bain. Detroit, MI: Apogee Books, 1990, cloth, p. 226. [biography]

J38.   "Kurtz, Katherine, 1944- . *Chronicles of Deryni*," in "Modern Fantasy for Adults, 1957-88," by Maxim Jakubowski, in *Fantasy Literature: A Reader's Guide*, edited by Neil Barron. New York & London: Garland Publishing Inc., 1990, cloth, p. 270. [critique]

J39.   "'What God Doth the Wizard Pray To': Neo-Pagan Witchcraft and Fantasy Fiction," by Carrol L. Fry, in *Extrapolation* 31 (Winter, 1990): 333-346. [critique]

J40.   "Kurtz, Katherine (Update)," in *Beacham's Popular Fiction, 1991 Update*, by Walton Beacham *et al.* Washington, DC: Beacham, 1991, paper, p. 711-716. [bio-bibliography]

J41.   "Kurtz, Katherine Irene," in *The International Authors and Writers Who's Who, Twelfth Edition*, ed. by Ernest Kay. Cambridge, England: International Biographical Centre, 1991, cloth, p. 491. [bio-bibliography]

J42.   "Kurtz, Katherine," in *Twentieth-Century Science-Fiction Writers, Third Edition*, edited by Noelle Watson and Paul Schellinger. Chicago and London: St. James Press, 1991, cloth, p. 458-459. [bio-bibliography]

J43.   "Kurtz, Katherine," in *The Writers Directory, 1992-94, Tenth Edition.* Chicago and London: St. James Press, 1991, cloth, p. 566. [bio-bibliography]

J44.   "Bridges: An Appreciation of Katherine Kurtz," by Andrew V. Phillips, in *Lunacon 1990 Program Book.* 1991, p. 9-10. [profile]

J. Secondary Sources

J45. "Kurtz, Katherine. *Lammas Night*," in *Supernatural Fiction for Teens: More Than 1300 Good Paperbacks to Read for Wonderment, Fear, and Fun, 2d Edition*, by Cosette Kies. Englewood, CO: Libraries Unlimited, 1992, paper, p. 98. [critique]

J46. *The Work of Katherine Kurtz: An Annotated Bibliography & Guide*, by Boden Clarke with Mary A. Burgess. Bibliographies of Modern Authors, No. 7. San Bernardino, CA: The Borgo Press, February 1993, 128 p., cloth. [bibliography]

   ab. San Bernardino, CA: The Borgo Press, February 1993, 128 p., trade paper.

J47. "Talking with Katherine Kurtz," by Jeffrey M. Elliot and Robert Reginald, in *Ibid.*, p. 83-116. [interview]

An adaptation of the 1980 Elliot interview with Kurtz (see K17), updated by Reginald, who posed additional questions, corrected anachronisms, and generally updated the original, with many new responses and corrections by Kurtz.

J48. "Kurtz, Katherine," by John Clute, in *The Science Fiction Encyclopedia, Second Edition*, edited by Peter Nicholls and John Clute. London: Little, Brown & Co. Ltd., 1993, cloth, p. . [critique]

   ab. *The Science Fiction Encyclopedia, Second Edition*, edited by Peter Nicholls and John Clute. New York: St. Martin's Press, 1993, cloth, p. .

K.

MISCELLANEA

K1.   PSEUDONYMS. Other than her birth name, Kurtz has used only one other penname, B. Fraser, on a series of articles on heraldry for her journal, *The Deryni Archives*. The pseudonym derived from Bevin Fraser, her identity in the Society for Creative Anachronism.

K2.   DEDICATIONS. The following books have been dedicated to Kurtz, in whole or in part:

  1.   *The Patrimony: A Horseclans Novel*, by Robert Adams. New York: A Signet Book, New American Library, April 1980, 184 p., paper. "This volume of Horseclans is dedicated to Poul Anderson and L. Sprague de Camp...and to two lovely and talent young ladies, C. J. Cherryh and Katherine Kurtz...."
  2.   *The Shining Paths: An Experiential Journal Through the Tree of Life*, by Dolores Ashcroft-Nowicki.   Wellingborough, Northamptonshire: Aquarian Press, 1983, 240 p., trade paper.

K3.   CAREER. Kurtz has worked at the following positions: Production Secretary, KOVR-TV, Sacramento, CA, 1967-1968; Technical Writer, Los Angeles Police Academy, 1969-1981, with the Civil Service ranks of Junior Administrative Assistant, Training Technician, and Senior Training Technician. Since 1981 Kurtz has been a full-time writer.

K4.   AGENTS. Kurtz has used the following agents: Russell Galen, at the Scott Meredith Literary Agency (1985-DATE).

K5.   MEMBERSHIPS. Kurtz belongs to the following organizations: Authors Guild; Science Fiction and Fantasy Writers of American, Inc.

K6.   CATALOGING.   In the Library of Congress classification scheme, Kurtz's main entry is "Kurtz, Katherine." Her permanent literature number is PS3561.U69; her bibliography number is Z8468.64.

QUOTH THE CRITICS

GENERAL COMMENTS

"I was excited to find out that Katherine Kurtz was going to be the Guest of Honor at Confusion this year. I owe her a big 'Thank You,' and would like to deliver it in person!

"It all started back in 1979, when Katherine was Guest of Honor at Marcon. In her remarks at the opening ceremonies, the very pretty and willowy Katherine said that she liked to talk to people, so no one should be shy about approaching her. I took that as a cue and arranged to do an interview with her in my room on Saturday afternoon. With other people in tow who were marvelous as both audience and participants, we spent nearly two hours talking about her life and the background of her Deryni world which Katherine shares so generously with her readers.

"Katherine's background is widely varied, as any reader of her works would know. Born in Florida, where she earned a B.S. degree in chemistry, she worked one summer at the Institute of Marine Studies in Miami between her junior and senior years of high school. The paper that resulted was submitted to the Westinghouse Science Talent Search and yielded a full science scholarship at the University of Miami (one of two given out annually). While at the University, Katherine shifted her interests from science to the humanities, although she did go into the medical program for a year. When she moved out to the West Coast, she got a job with the Los Angeles Police Department, working as an administrative assistant in the Narcotics Division (she earned a 99% on the qualifying exam, an almost unheard of figure: 'I didn't know it was supposed to be hard—nobody told me!' she said). From there she became a full-time civilian instructor in written and oral communication at the Police Academy, and developed an integrated multi-media training program.

"At the same time, Katherine also took courses at UCLA and eventually earned her M.A. in English history in 1971. She has occasionally returned to take other courses in subjects that interest her. During all of this Katherine wrote the first Deryni trilogy.

"Additionally, Katherine has been a member and Queen of the Caid Kingdom in the Society for Creative Anachronism, and with some of the *Star Trek* fans in the Los Angeles area managed to become an 'extra' in *Star Trek: The Motion Picture*. As is evident from her novels, she is interested in magic, Church and Medieval history, parapsychology and extrasensory powers, education and learning techniques, costuming, and discreet forms of warfare and intrigue. And who knows what else she has added to this list since I first talked to her eight years ago.

"Well, I could add that she has married, has moved to a castle in Ireland, and thus, I suppose, is learning castle upkeep and management firsthand. Add to that, then, caring for the manor grounds, maybe some farming, how to get along with the new neighbors, and...well, ask her yourself. Katherine still enjoys talking to fans about her books, about herself, about almost anything else. As for me, yes, I want to talk to her again; eight years is a long time, and we have a lot to catch up on. But mostly I want to thank her.

"At that Marcon so long ago, a new fan attended her first convention, specifically because Katherine Kurtz was the Guest of Honor. This new fan and I met and started a correspondence which continues today, although the distance between us has diminished. About three and a half years after that initial meeting, Maia Cowan and I got married.

"So, thank you, Katherine Kurtz! Because of you, I met my wife. Now you can add 'matchmaker' to your list of accomplishments!"

—George "Lan" Laskowski

"Kurtz's double trilogy [The Chronicles of the Deryni and The Legends of Camber of Culdi] is a many-leveled achievement. Simply as fantasy, it has much to offer its readers. Richly imaginative in its handling of magic and of a convincing secondary world, it is a satisfying structured fantasy quest. On reflection, however, it offers much more. As historical fantasy it is richly detailed concerning medieval life, especially the medieval church. Furthermore, it goes beyond historicity to a creative revisioning of the period it so concretely represents. In many of its thematic concerns, it offers a rewriting of history with a focus on women's issues. The usual metaphorical quest for meaning and identity at the heart of fantasy here reaches beyond the individual quester to women as a group, in particular those women who suffered from accusations of witchcraft. Deryni sorcery, a gift and yet a curse, reflects the repressed feminine side of human nature.

"The most prominent theme in these books, one which is not limited to the feminine, is the problem of prejudice. Because of their unique kind of 'difference' the Deryni serve as a far-reaching model of historical victims of prejudice. The prejudice that results from perceived differences of race or religion is intensified in the case of the Deryni because their difference is not readily visible. Although their psychic skills are racial in that they are biologically inherited, they are not immediately detectable. This inherited difference is also potentially either a boon to society or a threat, depending on how it is used. This ambivalence makes it even more feared. Since some of their skills are magical, they become readily associated with antireligious practices like witchcraft. Even Cinhil, who should know better, expects as he peeks into the tent on the morning of the battle to find some weird magic rite being performed, and is surprised to find that it is actually a celebration of the mass. The prejudice against this psychically gifted people also takes a social form, as when the members of the council deny the Deryni the right to own property or to hold office. In its extreme form this prejudice against the Deryni difference takes the form of genocide. In the last volume of the Camber series there are mass murders and executions, both of Deryni and suspected Deryni sympathizers.

"By making the fundamental 'difference' that marks the Deryni for discrimination, ostracism, and mistreatment simply a 'skill,' Kurtz captures the inherent absurdity in all prejudice. She also is concerned with the less obvious type of prejudice against an aspect of the human mind. In Western history, with its prevailing emphasis on logic and reason, the intuitive and the fanciful have been victims of prejudice. Whereas in some societies dreams are taken very seriously by people in positions of leadership, in ours dreams are scorned or relegated to psychiatric case histories. The society that represses and discriminates against the Deryni is prejudiced against those aspects of the mind that the Deryni represent, i.e., the intuitive, the visionary, the fanciful, the creatively magical.

"Another important theme is power, its use and abuse. The Deryni themselves illustrate the subject in the varying ways they use their own occult powers. The destructive use of Deryni skill is exhibited in several characters, including the murderous Charissa and the tyrannical Imre, but the hunger for power and the exploitation of others is practiced more pervasively by humans, exemplified in both religious and political leaders. Throughout these works the desire for power as such is offered as a negative goal. The power implicit in skill should be limited to helping others.

"Closely related to this attitude toward power is the notion of using one's gifts wisely. The principal example is Cinhil, who at the age of forty is asked to give up his chosen calling in order to fulfill his duty as the only living heir to the throne. Camber's dilemma is the opposite in that he must take on the identity of a clerical man in order to better fulfill his own determination to advise the reluctant king. For many, of course, any use of their talents might endanger their lives. Camber's decision to make proper use of his own talents leads him to sacrifice his identity for the sake of his king and country.

"The oppression of unorthodoxy is another theme that runs through the story. The older, more conservative bishops who represent the orthodox position of the church are eager to pronounce an anathema against the Deryni. Only a few of the younger bishops recognize the genuine spirituality inherent in the Deryni unorthodox magic. Just as Jews and witches in the Middle Ages were blamed for all sorts of natural disasters, Kurtz has the priests blaming Deryni black magic for the outbreak of the plague. The vacillation in public opinion and in church officialdom between conferring sainthood on Camber and denouncing him as a heretic illustrates the thin line between orthodox and unorthodox spirituality.

"Kurtz's description of the desecration of a chapel honoring Saint Camber vividly evokes the actual ransacking and destruction of monasteries during the Reformation period. So quickly and so totally does orthodoxy descend to unorthodoxy in time. 'Nor did they spare the Lady Chapel, with its cool, jewel-like panels of blue glass let into the walls, and its rich hangings;...Even the mosaicked hemisphere on which the statue had stood was attacked with club and mace...A torch was set to the once-exquisite wooden screen which had taken years to carve, and the fire cracked and blackened what the soldiers had spared and which would not burn'

(*CH*, p. 371). The passage reflects the author's love of medieval church architecture and ornamention as well.

"Paralleling the theme of orthodoxy is that of the two magics. Bishop Cullen once refers to the mass as 'this greatest magic' (*SC*, p. 95). With total respect Kurtz presents the rituals of Catholicism such as the mass as rich in transformation symbolism central to the concept of magic. In these works the two magics, the transcendental, liturgical magic of the church and the individual psychic magic of the Deryni reflect and confirm each other. They are complementary rather than conflicting. The magical Portal Transfer, for example, gains credibility by analogy to the parallel religious image of a dead man's soul sliding away from his body. Death is another kind of portal transfer. Kurtz avoids didacticism, but such parallels embody a lesson of respect for another's magic.

"Kurtz's two trilogies are a unique achievement in fantasy. Like many other women writers she stresses the depolarization of values and the renunciation of power, but unlike them she incorporates the theme of immortality. The feminism in her work is not, however, a matter of theme but of approach. In the framework of historical fantasy she revisions an historical period, the Middle Ages. On the social level the repression of the Deryni by church and state is equivalent to the repression of women and Jews in that period. Psychologically the repression is of those qualities traditionally regarded as feminine, such as intuition.

"Kurtz's style matures dramatically in the course of the trilogies. Although the first Deryni volumes suffer occasionally from banal language, the later books are beautifully written. The language becomes richer, more metaphorical, more rhythmic, and effectively modulated by biblical overtones. When, for example, Camber holds a dying friend in his arms, 'He felt the ethereal, detached sensation as the silver cord began to unravel and the ties of earth-binding were loosed' (*CH*, p. 478). Many of her finest touches of poetic language occur in descriptions of the moment of death: '...and then a nothingness which was pervaded by a blinding, incredibly beautiful light of all the colors of time' (*CH*, p. 296). But her descriptive powers are not limited to spiritual moments, for her physically detailed depiction of the horrors of war and execution is often both moving and shocking. Although almost totally neglected by scholars, *The Chronicles* and *The Legends* are rewarding reading."

—Charlotte Spivack

DERYNI RISING (1970)

"The first volume in Kurtz's high fantasy series, The Chronicles of the Deryni, tells the story of Kelson Haldane, the young king of Gwynedd, and his friends and protectors, Duke Alaric Morgan and Father Duncan MacLain. Morgan and Duncan are Deryni, members of an ancient race of sorcerers who have long been persecuted in the Eleven Kingdoms. When King Brion is slain by Charissa, another Deryni, those people in Gwynedd who hate and fear the Deryni rise up in rebellion against Kelson and his Deryni sympathies.

"At the same time, Charissa threatens not only his kingship but his very life. Morgan and Duncan have many harrowing and dangerous experiences as they work to help Kelson overcome the rebellious factions and avenge his father's death. At the coronation ceremony, all things come to a head as Kelson is revealed to have powers himself and Charissa challenges him to an arcane duel. Even though he is inexperienced in Deryni ways, with the help of his friends he manages to vanquish the wicked sorceress and is at last crowned King of Gwynedd.

"This is an exciting tale with an intricate plot peopled with fascinating and likable characters. Though some elements are familiar to us, such as the Church and its various rituals and traditions, the book can definitely be considered high fantasy. The setting is an imaginary land and the Deryni possess such qualities as mind-reading, healing by touch, and self-transportation. The Eleven Kingdoms and many of the characters are described in such rich and vivid detail that they are immediately recognizable. Kurtz also gives the Deryni a history that is frequently referred to and gives the story credence."
—Marshall B. Tymn, Kenneth J. Zahorski, Robert H. Boyer

DERYNI CHECKMATE (1972)

"This continuation of the saga of King Kelson of Gwynedd and the Deryni's fight for survival flows smoothly from the end of the first volume, *Deryni Rising*. The priests and a rabble of peasants grow in strength, and their opposition to those of Deryni heritage is now a fierce and mindless hatred focused on total destruction. Kelson's closest friends and advisors, Duke Alaric Morgan and Father Duncan MacLain, are relentlessly pursued by the Church and rebels alike as they strive to halt the mounting disquiet and prove that human and Deryni can live peacefully side by side.

"Gwynedd is also threatened with invasion by Wencit of Torenth, and unless the country can stand undivided by internal strife, it will surely be taken. A personal crisis for Duncan arises when he must reveal his Deryni powers in order to save Morgan from certain death. As priest and Deryni—states generally assumed to be irreconcilable—he is tortured by feelings of guilt. Finally, a council of bishops votes to excommunicate the two Deryni, and Kelson is faced with choosing between his country and his dearest friends. But, as this volume ends, he decides to ignore the excommunication order, and he, Duncan, and Morgan join forces in a last attempt to save their country.

"Kurtz has no problem maintaining the pace and excitement she established in *Deryni Rising*. She has the ability to introduce new characters and make them very interesting and real in a few short sentences. Such is the case with Kevin MacLain, his fiancée, Bronwyn Morgan, and the architect Rimmel, who harbors a secret passion for Bronwyn. Their tragic story is not essential to the main theme, but its inclusion further illustrates that the Deryni heritage is truly a two-edged sword. And the tragedy would not have the impact it does if the characters had not been developed as fully and carefully as any destined to live out the series.

"The persecution of the Deryni is an example of the continual struggle between good and evil often found in fantasy literature. But Kurtz adds a twist by not making all the Deryni good and all the humans evil. The evil is that some people hate and fear other people merely for what they are, and that there are always those who will take advantage of that prejudice."

—Marshall B. Tymn, Kenneth J. Zahorski, Robert H. Boyer

HIGH DERYNI (1973)

"In this third volume of the Chronicles of the Deryni, the leader of the rebel faction is finally persuaded to join forces with the King of Gwynedd against the invading forces of Wencit of Torenth. King Kelson, little more than a boy in years, is once again aided in this task by his close friends Alaric Morgan and Duncan MacLain. The three young Deryni are able to halt the growing wave of persecution against those of their heritage so the country can unite to face a truly evil enemy, who also happens to be Deryni. For although a corrupt Deryni has powers at his disposal that enable him to inflict more pain and torture than his human counterpart, like humans Deryni can be either good or bad. It is an individual choice that we observe many characters making throughout this story.

"As the two armies come face to face for the final battle, the Camberian Council makes a ruling that the victory will be decided by a duel arcane. It is to be fought with Deryni weapons by four from each side. But the ending has a twist that will surprise even the most perceptive reader. One of Wencit's trusted friends reveals his true identity and the duel is never fought. In the guise of Rhydon of Eastmarch, Stefan Coram is able to poison his supposed comrades and win the battle for Kelson and his supporters.

"*High Deryni* is even more exciting and spellbinding than its two predecessors. Perhaps the most interesting departure from the other books is the development of a love relationship between Morgan and the beautiful Richenda, Countess of Marley. It does not play a major role in the story line, but among other things it does give us some new insights into Morgan as a man. Richenda is a vibrant and welcome addition to a cast of characters that is dominated by males. She does for this book what Eowynn did for Tolkien's *Return of the King*. Some of the other major characters also continue to develop and grow. Kelson and Duncan come to terms with, respectively, their kingship and priesthood, and are able to reconcile these offices with their Deryni natures. Sean Lord Derry undergoes much personal pain and suffering at the hands of Wencit and emerges a stronger person. There are four appendices to help the reader sort out the various characters and places, a time line for the history of the Eleven Kingdoms, and an essay on the genetic basis for Deryni inheritance. The end of the story is not altogether happy, but this only serves to make *High Deryni* a very real tale."

—Marshall B. Tymn, Kenneth J. Zahorski, Robert H. Boyer

CAMBER OF CULDI (1976)

"*Camber of Culdi* introduces the reader to the country of Gwynedd, a medieval society peopled by two 'races,' the humans and the Deryni. The latter are human in form, but have advanced skills in magic. The king is a Deryni of a family which overthrew the previous human dynasty about eighty years before our story opens. King Imre is a spoiled brat who hasn't the faintest notion of how to govern, but is well-versed in the arts of intrigue, debauchery and drunkeness, with a little incest thrown in for spice. Truly, a villain you love to hate. He's so bad even his fellow Deryni can't stomach him any longer.

"Camber, Earl of Culdi, is a wealthy Deryni landowner who has retired from politics to devote himself to magical studies and being a benevolent grandfather to family and serfs alike. His oldest son is handling the court duties. However, when his second son, a priest in an order of warrior clergy, and his future son-in-law discover the surviving last heir of the old dynasty, Camber wants a look at the man. Maybe it is time to right old wrongs and get the despot off his throne.

"But the heir doesn't want to be king. He's quite happy where he is, thank you, and doesn't want his peaceful monk's life interrupted for anything so minor as the good of his country. Not that he has much say in the matter. Camber, backed by his family and a great many other citizens, are going to get their way or die in the attempt.

"The rest of the story deals with the intrigue coming to fruition through both human ideals and Deryni magic.

"Although the story up to this point has been fairly predictable, the characters are well-drawn and Kurtz's descriptions of this medieval-type society are vivid. Small details flesh out the reader's vision of what's occurring and where it's taking place. When Kurtz writes bleak and cold, the reader *feels* bleak and cold. Her efforts are marred only by occasional awkward sentence structures which leave the reader foundering in confusion.

"The reader who hates 'to be continued' as much as I should have the second book of the series at hand to leap into immediately. This one does not tie up all the loose ends, and leaves one with the feeling of having had the proverbial one peanut. However, it's well worth reading—if you consider it the appetizer of the meal."

—Kathleen Conat

"The events of this book take place some two hundred years prior to those in the first three Deryni chronicles. It is the story of Camber MacRorie and the part he and his family play in the restoration of the Haldane line to the throne of Gwynedd. Although Camber and his family are of Deryni blood and possess extrasensory powers, they are dismayed and angered by the actions of the current Deryni ruler. When they learn of the existence of a direct descendant of the previous human rulers, Camber, his son Joram, and their close friend Rhys Thuryn work to place Cinhil Haldane on the throne. They are hampered in their efforts not only by agents of Imre, the Deryni King, but also by the heir himself. Cinhil has lived the better part of his adult life as a cloistered monk, and is unwilling to abandon that role for one of a layman, let alone a king.

"As their treasonous deeds become more difficult to conceal, Camber and his family are forced to take the reluctant Cinhil into hiding, where they prepare for the day of final reckoning. Cinhil becomes resigned to his royal heritage, but it is not until the death of his infant son at the hands of one of Imre's men that he becomes wholeheartedly involved in the effort to overthrow the Festillic ruler. This is accomplished with the death of Imre and the disappearance of his sister.

"*Camber of Culdi* is carefully written to correspond with any reference made to this earlier time period in the other Deryni books. The characters are thoughtfully developed, from the despicable Imre to the wise Camber. But the most fascinating character is the elusive Cinhil Haldane. His struggle against his heritage, which changes to passive resistance and finally to willing acceptance, is skillfully portrayed and very believable. This story is also probably Kurtz's most somber to date. Her depiction of Cathan MacRorie's anguish and of Imre's despair after Cathan's murder is real enough to pierce the reader's soul."

—Marshall B. Tymn, Kenneth J. Zahorski, Robert H. Boyer

SAINT CAMBER (1978)

"This is the fifth of Kurtz's novels set in Gwynedd—the parallel-world of medieval Wales where magic is real—and it confirms her status as a master of epic fantasy. The novel is distinguished by fine characterization, meticulous detailing and magic that is believable and awesome because it is not too easy. While it has its share of action, there's more ceremony than sword play, since the focus of the book is the soul-testing dilemma faced by Camber of Culdi when he decides that the good of the kingdom requires him to exchange bodies with Alister Cullen when that knightly priest dies in battle. Trapped in his magical impersonation, he is made a bishop in his friend's place and must watch helplessly as his 'dead' self—Camber—is declared a saint. This is a gripping novel, dignified by serious moral issues and brightened with all the color of an imaginary world."

—*Publishers Weekly*

"This second book [in the Camber series] is better than the first, and faster paced. Having so meticulously set her background in the first novel, *Camber of Culdi*, Kurtz no longer feels the need for lengthy descriptions, and we get more plot development.

"King Cinhil, who has now ruled Gwynedd for approximately six months, is still not charmed with the idea of being king. His wife, who was Camber's ward, has given him a set of twins, but both are them are physically flawed, and Cinhil sees this as retribution from God for having given up his priestly vows. He and Camber aren't getting along, because Cinhil blames Camber, rightly, for forcing him into his current role. He is rapidly becoming fast friends with Alister Cullen, leader of the militant order of clergy, the Michaelines. But Alister is due to be made a bishop and sent far from the capital city.

"Gwynedd is about to be attacked by forces led by Imre's sister, Ariella, who fled during the coup and gave birth to Imre's incestuous child in neighboring Torenth (where the Deryni still rule). All is not well with our merry little band of court politicians.

"Cinhil's backers go to war against Ariella and her troops. In the fighting, Cullen is killed by the rebel princess herself, but manages to return the favor before drawing his last breath. Camber, coming upon the scene, realizes that his best link with Cinhil (Alister Cullen) is gone, and resolves, through the arts of Deryni shapechanging, to take his place.

"The rest of the book is involved with Camber's adjustments to his new role, and a close view of the religious structure and beliefs of Gwynedd. Although Cinhil's further adjustments to his rulership are mentioned, the focus is not on the king, but on the religious community and its role both in the personal lives of believers and in the secular community as a whole. This by no means makes it boring to read. On the contrary, Kurtz presents a richly woven tapestry of machinations and manipulations with an authenticity of motivation which entraps and intrigues the reader.

"Again, awkward sentence structure at times mars the storyline. Not enough of this occurs in one patch, however, to offset interest. The ending is much improved, tying up more ends satisfactorily, even while blatantly announcing there is more of this story yet to come."

—Kathleen Conat

"Volume II in the Chronicles of Camber, *Saint Camber* is the continuation of the story that revolves around Camber MacRorie, his family, friends, and foes. The action picks up almost immediately from the end of *Camber of Culdi*. The kingdom of Gwynedd has been reclaimed by the rightful human heir, Cinhil Haldane, with the aid of Camber and other supporters. But many problems still face the Deryni lord. Ariella, sister of the deposed ruler Imre and the mother of his child, has fled to nearby Torenth, where she plots with foreign Deryni powers to march against Gwynedd. At a time when Camber's advice and counsel is most needed by the immature king, Cinhil turns his back, blaming Camber for his lost priesthood and the deformities of his infant sons. He becomes progressively more bitter and Camber is at a loss as how to regain the King's trust.

"But the story takes a bizarre twist when Alister Cullen, a close friend and Vicar General of the Michaeline order, is slain in a battle with Ariella. Camber and his son Joram find Alister and Ariella both dead, and Camber comes to a startling decision. Alister had the trust and confidence of the King, and Camber realizes that the only way for him again to have a close relationship with Cinhil is to assume the shape of Alister and let it be Camber MacRorie who died. The shape-changing spell is difficult to work and maintain, but Camber manages to do it.

"As it becomes necessary to let more people in on the secret, Camber/Alister is increasingly apprehensive about the result if Cinhil or others should discover the truth. But a new problem arises when rumors about miracles supposedly performed by the dead Camber begin to circulate. Efforts on the part of Camber's family to stop the stories backfire, and the entire affair culminates in the petition of a new order of priests for the canonization of Camber. Horror-struck by these events, Camber/Alister and Joram try unsuccessfully to halt the canonization process.

"As each new piece of evidence is presented, the hierarchy of the Church becomes more convinced that Camber truly deserves sainthood. Even Cinhil is a witness to one of Camber's 'miracles,' and his unwilling testimony is the final proof needed to make St. Camber a reality.

"The pace of the Deryni chronicles is continued without a falter in this tale. But more gripping than the action and battles that take place is the deeper story of one man's sacrifice of his own identity to be able as someone else to help his kind and his country. Kurtz has used this theme before in *High Deryni*, when Stefan Coram reveals that he has been masquerading as Rhydon of Eastmarch for several years. Again, this is for a noble purpose and provides an interesting twist to the plot. One of the finest characterizations is that of Cinhil Haldane, the priest-king, whose struggle to be at peace with himself is a thought-provoking aspect of the story."

—Marshall B. Tymn, Kenneth J. Zahorski, Robert H. Boyer

CAMBER THE HERETIC (1981)

"This vast novel concludes the second trilogy in Kurtz' popular Deryni series, the story of the Deryni statesman and saint Camber of Culdi. It covers the period from the death of King Cinhil Haldane, through the beginning of open, ruthless persecution of the magically gifted Deryni by the humans, to Camber's own death. The first part of the book drags somewhat, as Kurtz fills in all the fine nuances of her large cast of characters and indulges a scholar's passion for the minutiae of medieval existence. The last third of the book—the stark tale of the persecutions—is the finest writing yet to come from this gifted storyteller. Recommended wherever the first first two volumes of the trilogy have been well received."

—Roland Green

LAMMAS NIGHT (1983)

"One of the strange-but-true items of information about Hitler's War—then known as World War II—is that Hitler believed implicitly in astrology, and England employed a corps of astrologers in order to know what the Führer believed and to keep one step ahead of what he might, advised by his astrologers, do for the war effort.

"There is also a recurrent rumor that the witch covens and occult groups of England, in that dark time when Hitler was planning invasion, got together to raise winds and bad weather which would stop the Germans—as they were also rumored to have done to defeat the Spanish Armada, raising the storm which destroyed it.

"Katherine Kurtz has taken these tales, and others, to create a splendid story of England in World War II—a time which 40 years has given the glamour of history. She has put together the story of Drake's Drum (which, when beaten in England's peril, supposedly would raise a force to defend his native land), and the persistent legends surrounding the death of such royal figures as William Rufus; Margaret Murray's 'The Divine King in England' suggests that, well into historical times, either the king or a specially appointed substitute for him was ritually sacrificed for the well-being of the land.

"The result is, of course, a wonderful thriller, with the quality of the very best occult and war novels. But it is more than this. It has that special quality of intense realism which leaves the reader wondering seriously, 'Can this be true?'

"Kurtz, better known for the fine series of 'Deryni' fantasy/historical novels, has done her homework well, visiting England and conferring with many of the occult groups who, perhaps, took part in these grand concerted efforts to save their land by raising unseen forces in defense of England.

"*Si non e vero, e ben trovato*...is an old expression roughly meaning, if it's not true, it makes a damned good story. Readers will have to make up their own minds about how true it may be; like all the fine artists in the field of fiction, Kurtz has left that to her readers for final judgment, while giving documentable evidence for the reader who cares to follow up on her research. On any level, this fine amalgam of thriller, folklore, war story, and wonderfully moving novel of tragedy, selfsacrifice, and human endeavor in what was justly called 'Britain's finest hour' will touch the heart of every Anglophile. It's certainly the best novel of its kind ever written.

"I have only one question for the publishers. Why was a novel of this caliber not published and promoted as a hardcover book? Many benighted readers and critics still refuse to take a book seriously if it is first published in soft covers. I implore the reader not to make that mistake."

—Marion Zimmer Bradley

"It has been said that in 1940 the Witches of England magically prevented Hitler from ever trying to cross the English Channel. Katherine Kurtz has developed this idea into a complex historical novel in which the 'occultists' (code word for Witches) re-enact the Celtic myth of the sacrifice of the sacred king, with Prince William as the willing sacrifice. In psychic (astral) travels to Germany, they uncover the horror of Hitler's *Thulegesellschaft* (the occult branch of Nazism) and infiltrate its ranks. And, as we all know, Hitler didn't invade. The characters in the book never know if their effort was in vain, whether Hitler would not have invaded anyway.

"This book is carefully labelled a 'novel,' and there is no doubt that that is its purpose. But the plot is so well constructed, and blends so well with recorded history, that it is hard *not* to believe. (I'm no historian, but I did do a couple of spot checks.)

"Regardless of truth, this is an enthralling tale masterfully weaving together psychic and political intrigue. A true Pagan novel, set in real-life history."

—Julie Ann

"*Lammas Night* is a re-issue of a 1983 by Katherine Kurtz, but I suspect that it was originally issued somewhere in the 3-digit range, given how many people I know who have looked for it, and how few people actually read it back in 1983. This is not the Deryni universe—it's set in Britain in 1940. A witches' coven is attempting to stop the psychic, as well as the physical, attacks by Nazi Germany on England. This isn't just any coven, however; the witches are also working in the highest echelons of the British military intelligence. Their plan? To 'protect' the British Isles by forming a grand coven of every witch and magic worker in Britain, and projecting a psychic shield around the island. This has been done before, but only at the cost of either a willing royal sacrifice or a willing substitute.

"Into this walks Prince William, the 'extra prince' of the Royal family. You won't find a Prince William among the sons of King George V in this world. However, in *Lammas Night* Prince William is both the twin brother of Prince John (who did exist, and who died at the age of 13), and a representation of what happens with 'extra' royals—Prince William feels useless, more of a public relations dummy than a human being. The Prince finds himself drawn into the covens' workings, and heads towards a fate which eerily parallels that of Prince George, Duke of Kent in real life. *Lammas Night* is an entertaining mixture of magic and intrigue."

—Laurie Sefton

THE BISHOP'S HEIR (1984)

"Readers of the two trilogies, The Deryni Chronicles and The Legends of Saint Camber, will welcome Kurtz's return to the kingdom of Gwynedd in this first volume of yet another trilogy, The Histories of King Kelson. *The Bishop's Heir* takes place two years after the end of *High Deryni*. Once again the stability of Gwynedd is threatened, this time by a Mearan princess, who claims to be the true heir to her secessionist province. She is joined by ex-Archbishop Loris, who has escaped from his confinement and who desires nothing less than the complete annihilation of the Deryni race. The story continues Kelson's exploration of the conflict between anti-Deryni fanatics and the Deryni, a race with inherent magical powers, while the gradual rediscovery of full Deryni powers and history seem likely to play an important part in the rest of the trilogy. The familiar characters from The Deryni Chronicles are all present; however, the focus shifts a bit to center on the young King Kelson and his new companion, Dhugal MacArdry, a highland clan chieftain.

"The action and pacing are somewhat uneven and many sections still display the creaky exposition and the laborious attention to detail which were characteristic of the earlier volumes. Intrigue, pomp, and pageantry, major features of the previous trilogies, are also present in abundance, and occasionally they bog down the plot. The problem of the almost unbelievable goodness of the 'good guys' remains; these men have small doubts, moments of indecision, and they make mistakes, but they are never forced to compromise their high ideals.

"Despite these flaws, I found myself enjoying immensely the return trip to Gwynedd. Kurtz has created a fascinating idealization of the Middle Ages, and infused it with a kind of magic one can truly believe in. Familiarity with the previous books is helpful, especially in emphasizing the motivation of certain characters, but not necessary. Libraries with Kurtz's other trilogies will want this volume. Recommended to teenage and adult lovers of 'high fantasy'."

—Diane K. Bauerle

THE KING'S JUSTICE (1985)

"The legions of fans of Ms. Kurtz's seven previous novels of this magical race will definitely want this newest addition to the Deryni universe. Readers unfamiliar with the Deryni could easily start here.

"The novel is set in the mythical kingdom of Gwynedd, a country akin to western Europe during the 10th or 11th century A.D., where the church (read Catholic Church) has a great deal of power and influence, and the magical Deryni blood 'taint' is feared and vigorously persecuted by the religious authorities. *Justice* deals primarily with the obstacles facing 17-year-old King Kelson and his Deryni advisors as they face an armed rebellion by royal pretenders in Meara. This is a self-contained adventure, although there are undercurrents of intrigue and character relationships continuing from Book One in the series, *The Bishop's Heir*, and unresolved events that surely will be tied up in the forthcoming *The Quest for Saint Camber*.

"This latest tale has all the ingredients that Deryni fans have come to love: political, religious, and magical maneuverings, hidden motives and anguish. Kurtz is one of those writers you either love or hate; there is no middle ground.

"Some readers may be put off by the heavily religious trappings of the Deryni Chronicles; others may be attracted. Magical rituals invoke the name of the one God and many of the saints, both real and fictional. Church functions and functionaries figure prominently in the plots.

"Kurtz also is highly descriptive with her prose, particularly of apparel:

Nigel removed a belt of metal placques set low on his hips, ducked out of the heavy, linked collar of his princely rank, then began unbuttoning a long, wine-colored overtunic with running lions intertwined around hem and cuffs.

although there is less in *Justice* than I remember from her previous books.

"All this helps to make her characters truly real. They have come so alive for me that I have become vocally angry or sad or excited about what they are doing or not doing to advance the plot. That doesn't happen with cardboard characters. Through these characters and descriptions, Gwynedd becomes a real world to the reader—where magic works according to specific rules. There is not much more you can ask of a fantasy novel.

"For less affluent readers, *The Bishop's Heir* is now out in paperback. You might want to begin there. Then read *The King's Justice*. I read it in one sitting—the best recommendation I can give."

—Michael J. Ducharme

THE DERYNI ARCHIVES (1986)

"This book is a collection of short stories based in the Deryni universe, collected from a number of sources (and with a number of diverse histories, as indicated in the author's notes).

"The stories cover a range in time from before the first Camber books up to just before *Deryni Rising*. Almost every one of the major characters are included in one story or another, and not a few loose ends are covered, notably the first meeting of Morgan and Derry, and the history of Bethane, who had figured in the deaths of Bronwyn and Kevin.

"The notes prefacing each story provide a rare and fascinating look into the author's mind as she develops each tale, and a tracing of the ideas and concepts as they are included in the stories. The reasons why each story was written, from doing a tribute to Andre Norton to providing a sale gimmick for a charity auction, are interesting in themselves.

"My favorite story of this collection is 'The Knighting of Derry,' about the acceptance of Sean Lord Derry into the service of Duke Morgan. Kurtz shows Morgan through Derry's sympathetic but intelligent eyes. This story shows the young squire's courage and sensibility when first encountering Morgan.

"There is also an appendix containing an index of characters and places mentioned in the stories, as well as a partial chronology. Also included are the origins of the Deryni saga, starting with the author's first rough notes following a vivid dream through the first novella through the initial proposal to Ballantine Books.

"This book is required reading for any fan of the Deryni series, and is recommended to any other reader as well."

—Terry O'Brien

THE QUEST FOR SAINT CAMBER (1986)

"In the final book of the second trilogy about Kelson, we see the king dealing with a number of elements carried over from the previous books, the main one being the lifting of the ban againt Deryni priests and the reinstallation of Duncan. The majority of the book is concerned with the tragic consequences to Kelson's search for the history of Saint Camber.

"During that search, Kelson and Dhugal are swept away in a raging torrent. Presuming that they are dead, Nigel assumes the Regency, declining for the moment to proclaim himself king. Conall, Nigel's eldest son and heir, has for the past few months been secretly training to achieve the Haldane powers (similar to those of the Deryni). When Nigel discovers this, Conall attacks him and places his father in a coma, thereby becoming Regent himself. He then takes Kelson's intended bride for himself.

"Meanwhile, Dhugal has rescued Kelson from death in an underground cavern. They spend several days searching for a way out, finally encountering a secluded group of followers of Saint Camber. Although at first mistrusting the King, the fanatics finally agree to help him.

"Kelson returns to the capital and reveals Conall's machinations. Conall forces the King to accept a duel arcane (mirroring the one with Charissa that accompanied his coronation), but is finally defeated and executed, although not without cost.

"Not all the questions have been answered. The Torenthi question is still open, and could still present Kelson with a future challenge. He must also find himself a bride, a task made more difficult by the presence of his mother, Jehana, who would save her son from his spiritual destruction by assuring that he has a proper (i.e., non-Deryni) spouse. He is also due for some troubling encounters from the Camberian Council. Finally, the enigmatic presence of Saint Camber in the epilogue raises many questions that are unanswered thus far.

"In each of her trilogies the author has avoided the pitfalls of writing lengthy series. Each novel can be read in its entirety almost alone, except for the necessary background information that the earlier books contain. Major plot elements are not left for the final book for resolution, but are resolved as encountered. For example, the Mearan rebellion begun in *The Bishop's Heir* was resolved in *The King's Justice*, thereby avoiding the let-down usually associated with the middle book of a trilogy.

"I'll be waiting expectantly and not-so-patiently for all future books of the Deryni sequence."

—Terry O'Brien

THE LEGACY OF LEHR (1986)

"Does murder, power, and politics sound like the basis for a Friday-night movie? Now add some interplanetary travel, a possible vampire, and some psychic blue cats, and you'll have *The Legacy of Lehr*, a new science-fiction novel by Katherine Kurtz.

"The luxury liner Valkyrie is forced to stop on Beta-Gemmorum III (the only planet in the galaxy that Lehr cats inhabit) to pick up four felines that are to be given as a political gift to the Imperial Prince. Almost immediately there is trouble for Wallis Hamilton and her husband, Mather Seton, the Prince's personal aides. Too many of the old superstitions about 'demon-cats' are surfacing as apparent truths. Passengers of the Valkyrie are found dead, each missing blood and holding a tuft of blue fur. What is the power of the cats? Can they somehow escape and return to their cages without being seen or touching the locks? Or is there a more disturbing possibility, is the lack of blood accountable to a...vampire?

"As the novel comes to a gripping conclusion, Kurtz proves that she can deal with the future as convincingly as she has dealt with the past in previous novels. Though the futuristic tale of *Lehr* is dramatically different from the historical fantasies that made her famous, it has many of the same recurring themes; she seems especially fascinated with the powers of the mind, and has a talent for making her fantasies seem like realities.

"Although her weakness is in developing relationships, her greatest talent is for creating strong characters. In *Lehr* one finds women such as Wallis Hamilton, whose capabilities and intelligence place her in high positions. In a literary genre dominated by male authors and their masculine protagonists, Kurtz provides a positive influence that other science-fiction writers should note."

—Andrea Byrne

"*Lehr* is primarily a locked room murder mystery set on a space ship. A luxury space liner is diverted to a backwater planet to pick up an emergency cargo—four bright blue, telepathic, noisy lions destined for the Emperor. Shortly, people start dying, their throats ripped out, a small amount of bright blue fur gripped in their dying grasp. The lions have been under guard the whole time, but it is obvious that somehow they're getting out of their cage, walking through the ship, killing people, and getting back in—past cameras, guards, and locked doors—all without being seen. Or is something else going on?

"Kurtz takes the story seriously enough to make it work, but with enough camp to keep it from getting overbearing. She throws in strange aliens (including one set whose main religious devil is a bright green, telepathic, noisy lion), vampires, religious fanatics, native rituals, and all sorts of other strange concepts without making you feel like she's playing games with the reader. When it all comes down to it, this book is well written and an enjoyable read. Byron Preiss, the packager, seems to have a winner with this new series, and I'm looking forward to future books."

—Chuq Von Rospach

THE HARROWING OF GWYNEDD (1989)

"There are obvious problems and pitfalls to the prequel novel. For example, a character may be newly dead by the time the 'future' novel occurs. The writer must then be able to keep the reader's interest while planning to do away with the person who might be the lead character. Also, when genealogies are provided in the original book, the writer has to keep to the schedule of births, deaths, and events. A hastily provided past is a deadly trap, while a well-thought-out past provides a good framework for prequels.

"Katherine Kurtz's *The Harrowing of Gwynedd* is a case in point. Anyone who has kept up with the Deryni novels knows the timetable of deaths after the 'death' of St. Camber. Especially evident is the death of Evaine, Camber's daughter. Also, the scope of Deryni persecutions has been alluded to in the 'future' novels, while the groundwork for these persecutions has been laid in the Camber series. Kurtz is able to work within these restrictions and still deliver an enthralling story.

"The storyline starts immediately after the 'death' of Camber. Camber's work, the stability and trust between human and Deryni in Gwynedd, has fallen apart under the pressure provided by a few evil men. These men feed off the fear of Deryni power, and they use their power as regents to mold the minds and hearts of the young princes left in their care. More horrifying than the physical torture is the

use of psychological and temporal means to destroy Deryni resistance. By using the
medieval Church, the cornerstone of society and ultimate authority, they destroy
Deryni by convincing them they are evil. The Church is held out as the wielder of
punishment and tool of salvation to the Deryni. By removing the Derynis' right to
exist, they have done much worse damage than mere physical slaughter.

"*The Harrowing of Gwynedd* is not an easy book to read. Kurtz ties you so
tightly to the fortunes of the Deryni, and the MacRories in particular, that every
transgression against them is a twisted knife in the gut. Because of the unbridled
jealousy of a few evil men, an entire race of people is tortured and destroyed. The
'good guys' don't win in the story, but from the struggle of good against evil comes
the power of the book."

—Laurie Sefton

"It's been a while since Katherine Kurtz wrote about the called the Deryni, so it is a
pleasure equal to finding a new Orson Scott Card novel to read and enjoy the first in
a new series of books about these uncontrollable wonder workers.

"The Deryni are still in deep trouble. Gwynedd is ruled by a weak boy
monarch who, in turn, is controlled by a succession of power-crazed regents intent
on finally destroying every vestige of Deryni influence. Events come to a head
when Bishop Alister Cullen, friend to human and warlock alike, dies and Camber of
Culdi, the venerable avatar who possessed his body and represents a font of knowledge for the beleaguered Deryni, also appears to be gone.

"Despite the weeks of official grieving in which the Bishop lies in state, his
body does not deteriorate, and it appears that he is trying to hold his human remains
together until his son and daughter can find a spell to bring him back from the dead.

"The book is a saga in the true sense of the word, with huge cast and appendices charting the history of Gwynedd which would put Tolkien to shame. It's a
rich brew of a read, but then Kurtz is a grand mistress of the high fantasy genre,
and still unchallenged by new writers in the field."

—John Gilbert

DERYNI MAGIC (1991)

"While this is set in her Deryni universe, it is not fiction *per se*. It's actually a
source book for the background and implementation of Deryni magic. There are
parts of the book which are copies out of previous Deryni books (and in one case, at
least twice), and parts which appear to either be drafts or short stories never before
seen. The book does give the Deryni fan a concrete and consistent base for how the
Deryni universe operates."

—Laurie Sefton

THE ADEPT (1991)

"When a wizard's sword is stolen from a museum in present-day Scotland, psychiatrist Sir Adam Sinclair is sure that the crime represents something serious. Through

a mutual acquaintance, he meets and befriends Peregrine Lovat, a troubled painter who is able to 'see' the past and future lives of his subjects. Sir Adam himself is the latest incarnation of the Adept, a spiritual force that battles evil, and he and Peregrine make a perfect team as they set out to discover who stole the sword—and why a 12th-century grave has been unearthed, freeing the revived corpse of Scotland's most noted magician, who then wanders into a bar in the dead of night. The sleuths determine that an evil cult seeks the magician's spell-book and hidden gold. Peregrine draws what he 'sees,' whether it's the location of the sword or the cult gathered at the graveside. Sir Adam's own mystical powers bring him close to the cult, but closer to mortal and spiritual danger. This is a fast-moving and suspenseful tale by an unusually adroit duo, and the ending promises more in the future."

—*Publishers Weekly*

THE LODGE OF THE LYNX (1992)

"A very clear-cut mystery, and a straightforward contemporary fantasy, *The Lodge of the Lynx* is the second novel by Kurtz and Harris featuring 'The Adept,' Adam Sinclair, Scottish lord, psychiatrist, expert in the occult, and mystic Master of the Hunt, a group of men and women dedicated to opposing the forces of darkness. The lynxes of the title are the dark forces in question, and they have taken to ritual murder, with Masons as their chosen victims. Detective Chief Inspector Noel McLeod calls in Sir Adam, who drags along his artist friend (and psychic protégé) Peregrine Lovat. Between the police and the official atmosphere of the Hunt, the style is one of an intense police-procedural—and the result is an even better mystery than its predecessor. The mystic elements seem more coherent and the characters better developed, and the pacing is superb, with a thrilling combination of grisly crimes, hair-breadth escapes, and the odd heartwarming moment."

—Carolyn Cushman

KING JAVAN'S YEAR (1992)

"Katherine Kurtz returns in fine form with her latest Deryni novel, *King Javan's Year*. Its title sums it up—the intrigue-ridden and tragically brief reign of a youthful king who seeks to end the persecution of the magic-wielding Deryni. Arrayed against him, and ultimately encompassing his death, are a motley crew of ecclesiastical and secular bigots, potentates, and troublemakers.

"Kurtz probably did more than any other American author to develop historically informed fantasy. Now in her maturity, she has slowed her output a trifle, but also has more than maintained the quality. Setting and characters are both vividly alive, and the pacing helps to keep readers turning every page.

"Please, do we have to wait three years for the next one?"

—Roland Green

TALKING WITH KATHERINE KURTZ

BY JEFFREY M. ELLIOT AND ROBERT REGINALD

Katherine Kurtz boasts a background as creative and varied as her fantasy nov-els—the four trilogies *Chronicles of the Deryni*, *Legends of Camber of Culdi*, *Histories of King Kelson*, *Heirs of Saint Camber*, plus *The Adept* series. One of the most popular series in print, the Deryni stories are sweeping tales of romance and sorcery set in the imaginary kingdom of Gwynedd. For both sequences, Ms. Kurtz draws on her background in medieval history and her study of religion and the oc-cult, weaving wondrous tales of magic and adventure.

The author was born in Coral Gables, Florida, during a hurricane—a whirlwind entry into the world which she likes to think was an omen of things to come. Kurtz's acquaintance with the written word began early in life. Indeed, her mother began reading to her from the time she was an infant in arms. She was a natural mimic, and on her second birthday, so she is told, she recited the entire poem of "Little Orphan Annie" for her grandparents, without a mistake or a hesita-tion. "I don't remember a time," recalls Kurtz, "when I couldn't read. I do know that I was already reading by the time I started school at age five, and was the top of my group, the Bluebirds (lower reading groups being Redbirds and Yellowbirds)."

Elementary school held few challenges for Kurtz. She used to take library books to school and hide them under her school books so that she could read what she wanted in class, to keep from getting bored. "I believe it was in the third grade," remembers Kurtz, "that I persuaded the librarians to let me have the run of the school library, instead of being confined to the picture books usually reserved for lower elementary school students. The clincher was the day I wanted to check out a copy of Walter Farley's *Black Stallion*, and they didn't want me to; they said it was too hard. I proceeded to open it and read, and they asked me a few questions about what I'd read. From that day on, I was allowed to check out as many books as I wanted, from whatever section I wanted. I also began reading out the local city library."

Kurtz read her first science fiction book in the fourth grade. It was a juve-nile called *Lodestar*. From then on, no science fiction book in the library was far from her reach. Even then, though, her tastes were geared toward humanistic sci-ence fiction, rather than hard science stories. According to the author, "Technology and bug-eyed monster stories never appealed to me, and still don't. I preferred ESP themes and strong characters. I also got away from short stories more and more. I've always felt that short stories, for the most part, constituted cruel and unusual punishment for the reader; because if they're good, you no sooner get going and they're over; and if they're bad, you've had to wade through all these little snippets of bad."

Kurtz's high school education was better than most. She graduated from Coral Gables High School, which at the time was one of the top five or so high schools in the country, especially in the sciences. She was a regional semi-finalist in the Westinghouse Science Talent Search her senior year, and that recognition won her a four-year science scholarship to the University of Miami, Florida. As she views it now: "I suppose you could say that the science award was my first really big break, because without that, I couldn't have afforded to go to college, and God knows what I'd be doing now."

The author's preoccupation with science didn't last very long, once she hit college. True, she graduated with a B.S. in Chemistry, and even attended medical school at the University of Miami for a year, but her heart had been lost to the humanities, and especially to history during her freshman year. As an undergraduate, she honed her writing and research skills on strict academic writing, so that by the time she came to the conscious choice to quit medical school and return to academic study, she had all the formal tools necessary for the transition. The short story which eventually became *Deryni Rising* was written during her senior year at the University of Miami. She wrote several *Star Trek* scripts the year following her withdrawal from medical school, mostly as learning exercises; and by the time she moved to California to continue her graduate studies in history, she was well enough along in the transitional process to begin writing serious fiction. The rest of her writing career is fairly well known, not to mention remarkable: a three-book contract with Ballantine Books on the first try, the initial books now well into multiple printings, with subsequent ones headed in that direction, and a faithful fan following which seems to be ensuring that the books will continue to be written and bought with gratifying regularity.

She settled in Ireland in 1986.

THE INTERVIEW

NOTE: Elliot's interview with Kurtz was originally conducted in 1979, and published in 1980 and 1982 (an expanded version). It was completely revised and updated by Reginald and Kurtz in November of 1992, with a number of additional questions being asked, and some previous responses revised.

ELLIOT: How did you become a writer?

KURTZ: I've always enjoyed writing. I started out as a reader. I was a voracious reader. I think I started reading when I was around four or five, and I've never stopped. I can remember in elementary school, which was *not* sufficient challenge for me, taking books to school and hiding them in my desk, lifting up the lid to read a page or two when the teacher wasn't looking; or hiding a novel under a textbook. And then, there were those innumerable nights when I'd read under the covers with a flashlight. I think most writers have gone through that stage. Anyway, having been brought up reading, I suppose it was natural that I reached the point when I thought, "I could write a story better than that." And eventually, I did. But in the meantime, I served my apprenticeship as an academic writer. Very early on in my student career, I learned the rudiments of good research practices and strict academic writing style—for example, never, never use a contraction. Or never, never write an incomplete sentence. Of course, a lot of these things are elements that have to be overcome when one switches to writing fiction. But the discipline was a good thing, I think. I despair of young writers today who haven't had the benefit of a strong background of grammar and spelling and punctuation. One can argue that such things don't matter in the face of true artistic genius, but I maintain that your young genius is never going to get his deathless prose read, if the potential editor has to wade through pages of sloppy, misspelled, non-grammatical prose. The material may be very good—but presentation is important, too. Most editors are just too busy to plod their way through something that is going to ruin his or her eyesight faster.than it's already getting ruined. The aspiring professional should be aware that first impressions *are* important.

ELLIOT: Many writers have been positively influenced in early life by a teacher or friend or family member who encouraged an early interest in literature. What about you?

KURTZ: As for my own development as a fiction writer, that was, in some respects, a long time in coming. My formal academic training was as a scientist. I was pre-med through four years of undergraduate study, and even started medical school. This kind of curriculum leaves one very little time for reading, much less writing, fiction. Fortunately, I had the good sense or the good fortune to take a very large number of courses in liberal arts disciplines, as well as sciences, even though I was working toward a B.S. degree. My professors in the humanities encouraged my creative endeavors; and one in particular, Mr. Carl Selle, even predicted that I would one day be a writer, not the physician I consciously thought I was going to be. You see, we were kindred spirits. He'd been where I was then. He'd started out as a medical student, too—though he only lasted one day, while I stayed for a year. When I quit medical school and went back to graduate school the following fall, I saw him during registration and told him what I was doing, that he'd been right. He didn't seem at all surprised. Unfortunately, he died before I actually began my writing career; but at least he knew I was back on the right track. I dedicated my first book, *Deryni Rising*, to him.

ELLIOT: For many years you worked for the Los Angeles Police Department producing instructional materials and films. Did this help or hinder your transition to a full-time career as an author?

KURTZ: I made the decision to write seriously, I suppose, during that year of medical school, when I really began to realize that my creative time was going to be curtailed more and more over the next few years. And then, in that next year, while I worked full-time and went to graduate school part-time to recoup my finances, I really began working on my fiction in earnest. I don't know when I made the decision to make the writing come first. I suppose that evolved over a long period of time, since I worked full-time at another job for over a decade while building my reputation as a writer. The most difficult decision was breaking completely with the world of salaries and shifting to writing full-time. It was simultaneously exciting and scary to consider living on a six-month income schedule instead of an every-two-weeks one, but in retrospect I think I made the break at about the right time.

REGINALD: Then came an even larger break, the move to Ireland in 1986, and the purchase of a manor house there. Why did you leave the United States?

KURTZ: There were a number of factors that contributed to the move. First of all, my husband and I had fallen in love with the idea of living in a castle, when we were on our wedding trip in 1983. We would have preferred a Scottish castle, but potential U.K. tax liability made that impractical. However, we kept coming back to that part of the world on our holidays, and wishing we didn't have to go back to California. Meanwhile, Anne McCaffrey reminded us of the tax advantages for artists living in Ireland; writers pay no Irish income tax on earnings derived from writing, and Americans get a slight tax break from the U.S. government for living overseas. (Not that one gets rich on tax savings; they just about balance out the higher cost of living.)

There was also the fact that our son was rapidly approaching the transition from elementary school to secondary school, and the public school situation in Southern California was looking more and more dismal. Aside from the obvious appeal that a European move held for Scott and me, the opportunity for Cameron to have a more traditional European education offered decided advantages. (He's just finished the equivalent of high school and begun college studies at Derby University in the U.K., and we're delighted with the poised and polished young gentleman he's becoming.)

REGINALD: How difficult has the move been, personally and professionally?

KURTZ: There haven't been any particular hardships that I can recall. Telephones work trans-Atlantic, though our phone bills are sometimes appalling. The mail usually works—when we aren't having a postal strike. (We've had two or three since moving here; the most recent lasted *six weeks*!) Fax machines have made our lives infinitely easier. After more than six years in Ireland, we've pretty much figured out how everything works, and find that the few annoyances we've had to resolve are much the same as the glitches one encounters living anywhere.

The most irritating initial difficulties were the same as if we'd simply moved to another city in the U.S.: the administrivia of setting up new bank accounts, utility accounts, health insurance, etc., and then the more prosaic tasks of finding new doctors, dentists, optometrists, plumbers, and the like. This may sound silly, but my personally most frustrating thing was finding someone to cut my hair the way I wanted. My first Dublin haircut was an absolute *disaster*, quite possibly the single worst haircut I've ever had in my adult life. Fortunately, hair does grow out fairly quickly, and I soon found someone I could train to do it the way I wanted. For the most part, though, we've slotted into the local environment very well, with minimum hassles. At this point, we'd find it very difficult to move back to the U.S.; and I find that each time I do return, it's diverged that much more from what it was when we left in 1986.

REGINALD: Clearly you enjoy living overseas. Do you find the people in the British Isles closer in spirit and culture to the world of Gwynedd?

KURTZ: I don't know how much closer they are—the area certainly has more similarities—but we're definitely closer to the world of Adam Sinclair, the protagonist of my new Scottish series. Back in California, we could only dabble in Scottish activities—Scottish country dancing, Highland games, and the like—and a few chivalric organizations. Now those kinds of activities are regular fixtures of our lives rather than occasional weekend anomalies. We live in a one hundred fifty-year-old gothic revival house that looks like a castle. One of our neighbors is an earl. We attend Clan MacMillan events up by Glasgow, where our Chief lives. One of our dearest friends here in Dublin is a man who, if Ireland still had a king, would be High King of Ireland; his family traces back in the direct male line to about the third century, acknowledged as the oldest royal house in all of Europe. None of this would be happening in California.

ELLIOT: Why the interest in things medieval? What's so fascinating about this particular period?

KURTZ: Oddly enough, I never had any real interest in the Middle Ages, historically speaking, until I hit college; and I don't know that it would have happened then if I hadn't been in an honors humanities program. Somehow, public school education manages to kill history for most kids by turning it into a dull, boring compendium of dates and facts. The way most history is taught, one would never know that it's about real people who lived and loved and created and thought—not just battles and wars and reigns of kings. In any case, I encountered a very uncommon professor the second semester of my freshman year. His name was John Knoblock, and he was and is a professor of philosophy at the University of Miami. He was the first true genius I'd ever met; at that time, he was about twenty-two or twenty-three, with a newly-minted Ph.D. in Oriental Philosophy and Art. He was also a proponent of the then-new concept of teaching history and all the other areas covered in the humanities through an integrated approach.

The time period that we covered was from the fall of the Roman Empire up to the Renaissance—but it wasn't a compendium of boring dates and facts—not at all. We studied the art, the architecture, the music, the poetry, the religion—all presented so that each area related to the other. He would bring in slides illustrating the points of architecture, for example, and ask us to tell him whether a window was Romanesque or Gothic, and why.

For example, he taught us about the feature of later artwork which he called "the Renaissance point." Take a look at almost any Renaissance painting, especially if it shows more than one person—religious themes are particularly good for this—and you'll notice that all of the lesser characters are pointing at whatever it is that's the center of attention in the painting: the crucified Christ, Pilate washing his hands, the Virgin Mary holding the Child. This was indicative of the tenor of the times, that if the artist didn't make sure you noticed the subject of the painting by having the people point at it, you might not get it. And these characters would go into all kinds of weird poses, uncomfortable and sometimes anatomically dubious ones, to get that finger pointing at the most important person.

But I think it was the architecture that really pulled me into medieval history. That may sound strange, but consider that architecture reflects the needs and the ways of thinking of the people. Church architecture, for example, went from the old Roman basilica form to the basic Romanesque design, sturdy and solid (to protect against the barbarian incursions), and on to the more soaring Gothic period, as life became stable and Man was able to have the time to turn his thoughts to God, instead of just worrying so much about mere survival. By the Gothic period, just prior to the true Renaissance, we have the flourishing of the cult of the Virgin, which also contributed to the whole troubadour-trouvère movement. (You didn't think *all* of those troubadour songs and lays were dedicated to mortal women, did you?)

Anyway, getting into the architecture and its whys and wherefores got me into the philosophy and religion. And, as anyone knows who has read the Deryni books, that became a major interest for me in the coming years—and still is. As Henry II puts it in *Becket*, I became involved in the *aesthetics* of the Church; and, gradually, this intellectual fascination with that whole mythos became something far more spiritual.

Nowadays, I read straight history and philosophy and religion for pleasure, as much as I read fiction—probably more so. I'm especially fascinated by the way Man's search for Deity has taken so many forms, and how the whole concept, in all its differences of belief and practice, somehow dovetails in a coherent whole. I don't think that any religion with a positive orientation is basically in conflict with any other one of like nature; I don't think there's any one right, true religion, either. Each person has to find his God—or Goddess—in his or her own way; and that Deity is going to be a little different for each person, regardless of the fact that it may be possible and comforting to band together with other people of similar beliefs for public celebration.

Religion—one's relation to the Creative Force—has to be a very personal thing. It isn't something that can be dictated by someone else—though formal religion can certainly suggest various frameworks within which to structure one's belief system. This may sound like a bit of contradiction, considering the role the Church plays in the Deryni world, but if you'll think about it, you'll realize that most of the characters who consider themselves religious have a definite and personal way of looking at the Church. They choose to operate within the general framework most of the time, but they have different ways of thinking on an individual basis. Camber's God, for example, is silent a great deal of the time—or maybe Camber just isn't listening on the proper frequency—but He is basically an understanding and forgiving God. Cinhil's God, on the other hand, is wrathful and punishing. After all, didn't He make Cinhil's son Javan deformed, with that clubfoot as a sign of His displeasure at Cinhil leaving His priesthood? That's what Cinhil thinks, anyway.

REGINALD: You obviously do have some experience in this area. From your writing, I would assume that you started life as a mainstream Roman Catholic.

KURTZ: Actually, I was brought up in a Protestant church, the Disciples of Christ, and I converted to the Roman Catholic Church when I was twenty-one. I can see now that part of what I was looking for—and found—in the Roman Church was the rich ritual tapestry against which the Christian faith is expressed; and, of course, this appealed to the trained historian in me. But once the usual convert shock began to wear off, it wasn't long before my Protestant upbringing began to point up basic incompatibilities with some of the tenets of the church I had lately embraced. All this was happening at about the time I started writing, so my depiction of the medieval church in Gwynedd was colored by my perceptions of what was both right and wrong about the Roman Catholic Church in our own universe. Nowadays, I would say that the Anglican Communion probably offers the most flexible mainstream framework in which to explore and grow in my own spirituality.

REGINALD: Your depiction of religious beliefs and practices in the Deryni books is one of the more compelling aspects of your fiction. Men and women believe or disbelieve and use or abuse the Church—and the Church herself interfaces with the state—in a manner starkly reflective of actual Church-state relations during the middle ages, when religion and politics were always inseparable.

KURTZ: This is one of those facets of history that most writers, especially in the fantasy field, have chosen to ignore—that religion and politics *were* essentially inseparable during the medieval and renaissance periods (which is the general milieu in which most of those writing fantasy set our tales). For that matter, most authors have mostly chosen to ignore any but the most superficial treatment of religious themes. Perhaps this comes partly of the fact that few fantasy writers have the historical background to handle this kind of synthesis. (They probably went to the schools that taught history as dates of battles and reigns of kings.)

I think this reticence to work with religious themes also comes partly from the general tendency in our present Western culture not to be particularly religious—which is not to say *irreligious*. Spirituality just does not seem to be a high priority in the general mainstream, and most people find it uncomfortable even to talk about it, much less write about it. To write about it convincingly, one has to have had at least some experience of it, I think. And one also has to have good instincts in how deep to go, to avoid bogging down the story and therefore failing in one's prime directive as a writer, which is to tell a good story and entertain. The line between preaching and being a catalyst to make the reader think can be very slender.

REGINALD: Yet the Church you depict is also different in several very significant ways from the Roman Catholic Church of medieval Europe. For example, the hierarchy of Gwynedd is self-governing and independent of external control, in the same way that the Orthodox churches of past and present Europe eschew any interference from Rome (or from each other). This clearly reflects your own personal beliefs, but it also subtly colors the workings of the stories.

KURTZ: That's certainly true. Aside from having to allow for and justify the existence of magic in the Deryni universe, the Church that began to emerge reflected some of my perceptions of how the ideal Church ought to be, wedding the aesthetic framework of High Church Roman Catholic practice to the more flexible collegiate structure I began depicting in the early books. I quickly established, for example, that there was no Pope and there were no Cardinals—much though I would love to have been able to have a character addressed as "Your Eminence." The dual primacies of Valoret and Rhemuth are a close parallel to Canterbury and York, and there are other similarities to the internal structure of the Church of England.

The other big difference—and this is one about which I was beginning to feel very strongly in the real world—is that the Christianity practiced by the main characters of the Deryni world (as opposed to the "Church-ianity" practiced by some of the less savory characters, and by far too many religious leaders of today) is devoid of most of the gloom and doom and guilt that seems to me to be the stumbling block in many of our present mainstream churches. One of the important catalysts in my own spiritual quest was my growing conviction that dwelling on such negative issues was not constructive or conducive to spiritual growth. So the positive depictions of spirituality in the books reflect a theology of joy rather than guilt.

REGINALD: Returning to the bishops, the history of Gwynedd implies that there was a time when the Church and its ruling Archbishops were controlled by an external body, as happened in real-life Europe. When did the Church of Gwynedd attain its independence, and why?

KURTZ: I haven't yet pinned down the exact time and circumstances of the split, but I've always had in the back of my mind that it probably occurred around the time of the Synod of Whitby in 664, when the English Church bowed to Roman practice and adopted the Roman means of reckoning the date of Easter, also abandoning the older Celtic practices that had characterized Christianity in Britain up until that time. However it happened, Gwynedd's church did end up with an internal structure that is closer to Canterbury than to Rome. Interestingly enough, Orthodox practice permeated the lands to the east of Gwynedd, with Moorish seasoning later on. We've seen hints of this eastern influence in several books, in conjunction with envoys from Torenth, and we'll see further and more detailed examinations of some of the differences when *The Captive Kings* takes us to the court of Prince Mark (or Marek) of Festil, whose church is Orthodox.

ELLIOT: Your academic training, including a Master of Arts degree in Medieval English History from the University of California, Los Angeles, clearly has helped prepare you for a career as a fantasy writer.

KURTZ: I had actually started writing epic fantasy long before I started my graduate work at UCLA, so I don't think it was so much a matter of my M.A. work "preparing" me in that area, as it was good leavening along the way, since it continued to hone my research skills and exposed me to actual medieval records in greater depth than I would have managed on my own.

My graduate seminar project, for example, involved translating the Hundred Rolls from Bedford County in England. These related to an inquiry conducted by Edward I in 1274, when he returned from the Crusades to find out what his ministers and Crown officers had been doing with his country while he was absent. The records I was working with were in medieval Latin, and done in an abbreviated form, which meant that you had to expand each contraction to its full Latin form before you could ever begin translating—and my Latin, at that point, was limited to what I'd learned from Church Latin.

Fortunately, much of the wording was somewhat formulized—there were charges brought against sheriffs and other Crown officials by the Hundreds, or sections of the country—and so it was fairly easy going once I'd mastered the abbreviations and the formula phrases. I came up with a fascinating picture of local corruption at various levels of government that I'd love to follow up someday by finding the rest of the records about this inquiry.

These were only the charges; I never got to see the other side. I do know that there's a fascinating historical novel in there someplace. I'd call it *The Sheriff*, and it would tell of this medieval sheriff who's been taking a little on the side and turning his head while his subordinates rip the people off, who suddenly realizes that the King is coming home and the sheriff is going to have to answer for what he's done. One of these days, in my copious spare time...

REGINALD: Very little is mentioned in the existing books of the early Haldanes (although their names are known, and one was apparently canonized), or of the founding of Gwynedd as a unified state. Augarin, the first Haldane, became High King of Gwynedd at the age of twenty-one in the year 645. Who was he before being anointed monarch, and what was the political and religious structure of the region like before the kingdom was founded? Will you ever explore this murky period in greater detail?

KURTZ: I've touched on a little of this early history in what little I've revealed so far about Orin and Jodotha. That would be a logical period to explore, but having said that, I don't know that I will, in any great detail, because the cat's already out of the bag in several important points. That's one of the hazards of succumbing to the temptation to drop tidbits of earlier history into a story. I *have* considered writing about Bearand and how he became a saint. And there's certainly a novel—or two, or three—about Augarin's founding of a unified Gwynedd. (Notice how that ties in with the date for Whitby?)

REGINALD: Did the Haldanes always have their potential for magic, or was this a development inaugurated with King Cinhil?

KURTZ: If the potential to assume Deryni-like powers is genetic, and this predisposition became fixed in the Haldane bloodline, then I would have to say that such a potential probably was always there—or at least was present from a very early time. I suspect that among Deryni schooled in the ancient arcana, much of which had been lost with the Airsid, there was at least a mythic tradition that Deryni powers had been put on select humans in the past; I don't think Camber would have thought of trying it if he hadn't some inkling that it was possible, at least in theory. It then fell to him and Evaine actually to test Cinhil to see if the potential appeared to be there—and then to catalyze that potential, essentially making Cinhil a Deryni like themselves. It's also possible that in the early days of the Haldanes, individual Deryni worked with individual Haldanes to catalyze at least some of the rudimentary Deryni powers, like Truth Reading. However, I don't think it became a familial connection until Cinhil.

ELLIOT: In other interviews you've mentioned Frank Herbert and his classic novel, *Dune*, as a positive influence.

KURTZ: I think what impressed me most about *Dune* at the time was the deft handling of characterization. I studied the way Herbert made his characters interact, how he wove together dialogue and action so that it flowed. There are very few slow spots in *Dune*, even when the characters are only talking. He had a very visual style in that book, and that was the way I wanted to write. I actually took apart a few of his scenes and analyzed them for this unique blend of talk and action which was successful for him in that particular book, so that I could figure out how he did it. I don't think I've ever done that with any other book, at least in writing, though there will be scenes here and there that I'll stop to re-read, to appreciate the artistry which makes a particular scene outstandingly successful.

But Herbert was only a jumping-off point, so far as learning that particular lesson. Far more useful, in terms of sheer craftsmanship, was writing *Star Trek* scripts back in 1968—and I heartily recommend this kind of exercise to any writer who's still trying to perfect his or her dialogue and pacing sense. The idea is to take a television series that you particularly like—*Star Trek* was ideal, since it had very strongly realized characters and a good, solid universe to work with—and to write a sample script for it. Format is not particularly important for the exercise—though if you pick a show that's going to be on the air for a while, there's always the chance (granted, slim) that you might be able to sell the script.

What *is* important is that: first, you have to fit your story into a somewhat artificial but disciplined structure of a teaser and four approximately equal length acts, each ending on a cliffhanger or other note that will make the viewer want to come back after the commercials (the same principle applies to chapter endings); and second, you already know how the characters talk, how they phrase things, so you can worry about writing believable dialogue which will carry your plot, instead of having also to worry about whether the characters will hold together. (It can be extremely difficult to keep all the points in mind at once, when you're just starting out; hence, you concentrate on juggling just a few things, at first.) From there, it's much easier to ease into writing one's own material, with original characters and universes.

ELLIOT: Unlike most writers, you achieved professional status almost overnight, getting an immediate offer from Ballantine Books with your first submission.

KURTZ: I guess I was too naive to realize that people don't sell three-book contracts their first time out. I had written a short story, "Lords of Sorandor," while I was still in college, and when I came to California, I started toying with the idea of expanding it into a novel. When I went to Baycon, the World Science Fiction Convention in Oakland in 1968—my first science fiction convention ever—I met a man named Stephen Whitfield, who had written the very successful *The Making of Star Trek* for Ballantine Books.

We got to talking, and I told him about my idea, and he said, "Hey, Ballantine is just beginning to look for original fantasy for their new Adult Fantasy series. Your idea sounds like it would be perfect. But don't write one book; write a trilogy." "You've got to be kidding," I said. "I haven't even written one, and you want me to write three?" "No problem," he replied. "What you do is, you write the first few chapters of the first book, with a page per chapter outline of the rest, and then you write a paragraph or so about each of the other two books. I'll tell Betty Ballantine to expect it."

Well, after several gulps, and many questions, all delivered in a very small, timid voice, I decided that maybe I could do it, after all. I didn't have enough experience to realize that the odds were almost astronomical against such a thing succeeding. So I wrote my outline and my sample chapters and I sent them off—and two weeks later, got back that magical letter from Ballantine saying, "Hey, we really love your idea, and how does a contract for three books sound, with thus-and-so terms?" Talk about being blown away.

Anyway, I accepted—and then settled down and began to work in earnest on *Deryni Rising*. It was well-received, especially for a first novel, and I continued working on *Deryni Checkmate* and *High Deryni*. By the time those were finished, I had begun to establish a small, but loyal, following among fantasy and science fiction readers. And when I started the Camber Trilogy, things really started to take off. When the third and final Camber book, *Camber the Heretic*, was published, the del Reys and I mapped out at least another six books in the Deryni universe. The sixth of these is now nearing completion late in 1992, and I have another four firmly in mind for the remainder of the decade.

ELLIOT: Would you be a better writer today had you been required to serve a longer apprenticeship?

KURTZ: I think my experience has generally been a positive thing. There are still times, though, when I sort of stand back and look at how far I've come and think, "Wow, is this really me?" Though I had to work full-time at another job while I got myself established as an author, I still am in the unusual position of actually making a living doing what I love to do—and unfortunately, not too many people are able to do that. I hope I will always be able to do what I love to do—writing my own things full-time.

Plunging right into things has been a good training ground, I think; I've just not had it as public as some other writers, since I don't do short stories, as a rule. My first one, "Swords Against the Marluk," appeared in *Flashing Swords #4*, but that's really part of a novel that I'll finally be getting around to in the next few years. I think that authors who go the short story route get much more accustomed to the chanciness to writing. A novelist does his or her work in much larger chunks, so there's more time to work out glitches and more chance that a good editor will catch you before you go to press and make you fix the awful things that might get through in a short story.

I'm not knocking short stories; I just don't care for them. I don't particularly like to read them, because just when a story starts getting good, it's over. I'm not that keen on writing them, either. Perhaps it's lack of discipline, but I find it very difficult to confine myself to that short a format. You may have noticed that I tend to write long novels. I feel too constricted by having to squash down my ideas. So I avoid writing short stories unless a whopping good idea comes to mind, made for the short story format. I find it almost impossible to just sit down and say, "Today I'm going to write a good story."

But back to the notion of apprenticeship—I've had my failures like anyone else, though thus far, I've usually been able to salvage apparently dead projects after letting them lie fallow for a few years. (After all, they don't eat anything sitting in a file cabinet.) One notable resurrection was a short story that I wrote as a favor to a friend, and then he didn't like it for the anthology he was putting together. It eventually became "A Tinkling of Fairybells," in Lester del Rey's very successful fantasy anthology, *Once Upon a Time*. (Part of the reason it didn't work the first time was because I'd tried to set it in a science fiction background, with the fairy as an alien. The inspiration for the story was drawn from a historical citation in the Venerable Bede.) Another "save" was a science fiction novel that I'd written back in the seventies, to a publisher's formula, and which, even after a major rewrite, didn't match the formula which the publisher *then* said was what we'd agreed on. It languished in one of my file drawers for years, until I found time to rewrite it the way it should have been done the first time around. Walker & Co. published it as part of their Millennium series in 1986 as *The Legacy of Lehr*, and it was cited by VOYA (Voice of Youth Advocates) in Best Science Fiction Titles of 1986. Like all my other titles, it's still in print. I suppose the moral of this story is, never throw anything away.

ELLIOT: You've described your particular brand of writing as "historical fantasy." How does it differ from what is commonly called "sword-and-sorcery fiction?"

KURTZ: I would describe "historical fantasy" as fiction which is set in a universe which closely corresponds to our own history, so far as sociological and religious background is concerned. In the Deryni books, I've tried to be very careful to give a real historical flavor to what I've written, drawing very heavily on my background as a cultural historian and trying to instruct as well as entertain. Very much of what I talk about, in terms of horses, falconry, sailing ships, food, armor, costume, etc., is drawn from our own historical background. The saints I mention, for example, are all pre-Tenth Century, or else they're made up. When I ordained Camber in *Saint Camber*, I adapted the ritual from an actual ceremony contemporary with the time.

I will also occasionally make changes on the technological level, such as giving Morgan's ship *Rhaffalia* a jib, which really wasn't developed until several hundred years later in our own world. When these anomalies occur, I try to give a plausible explanation for the difference. In a way, my Deryni world is an alternate or parallel of our own, with the divergence probably having occurred about the Fifth or Sixth Century.

Regular fantasy by contrast usually does not pretend to parallel our own history, except in the broadest sense. It tends to be more fairy tale medieval, for the most part, though it may draw heavily on mythological background of various cultures. And sword-and-sorcery is even more eclectic, tending toward more action and less characterization, in general, with magic that may be almost entirely of the hocus-pocus variety and inhabited by creatures which never

walked the world we know, except, perhaps, in nightmares. I think that characterization and internalization are important to the kind of fiction that I like to
read, and I think my writing shows this. Regular fantasy and sword-and-sorcery
tend not to stress these points as much as I would like. I suppose that's one reason I started writing my own. Many writers get their start writing out of sheer
preservation, because they can't find enough to read of the type they want.

ELLIOT: How extensively do you draw on history in your fantasy, both for plot
ideas and story details? What does history enable you to do as a writer that intuition doesn't?

KURTZ: As a historian, I'm convinced that we can and should learn from our
history, both the mistakes and the successes. But if a person hasn't studied history except as the series of dates and battles and royal reigns, then he may not be
aware of the valuable lessons to be learned from history. So, I am constantly on
the lookout for points of history that have relevance today, and for those connections of philosophy which are universally valid, regardless of the outward trappings. Handled skillfully, these can be both entertaining and enlightening experiences for the reader, not to mention the writer who puts them all together. I
learn things from every book I write. The research and the bringing together of
all the elements are half the fun of creating. As for intuition, that is often the
catalyst which takes two or three only possibly related elements and from them
synthesizes a new way of looking at something. Sometimes the characters themselves take the elements and forge something I wasn't expecting. Something
magical happens when your characters start showing up at your story confer-
ences with yourself. The first time Camber looked over my shoulder, I nearly
fell out of my chair. Javan, Cinhil's middle son, did that just the other night.

ELLIOT: One would imagine from work that you read and write Latin quite flu-
ently. The Deryni fantasies make superb use of Latin terminology, but not to
excess. How do you know when to stop, when you're approaching overkill?
What function does Latin serve in your fiction?

KURTZ: I fake Latin very well. Most of the Latin used in the books is taken directly from the Latin Missal or other liturgical sources. I do read Latin reason-
ably well for the purposes of translating old records, but the rest comes unnatu-
rally. I also have several priest friends who bail me out from time to time.
(They like the books, by the way.) The purpose of using the Latin in the first
place is partially to give the flavor of the times—after all, the medieval Church
was a great, overshadowing influence on all walks of life in the real Middle
Ages.

I try to maintain a balance between enough and too much of anything. In
the case of a strange word probably unfamiliar to my audience, I try to use it in
a context that will give the reader an idea of what it means. Then, if he looks it
up, that's even better. But at least I've planted another word in his unconscious,

and hopefully he's going to be the richer for it. All human endeavor can enrich others of the race. Even negative human acts can instruct and give us a better appreciation for positive human values.

REGINALD: In medieval Europe, Latin was the *lingua franca* of diplomacy, religion, and sometimes of commerce. Is that true in Gwynedd? I've also noticed occasional French phrases and names; even in the royal house of Haldane, King Brion's uncle is Prince Richard.

KURTZ: Latin certainly plays an important part in Gwynedd. I think it's the only language I've really identified by name. I've gone under the assumption that if the world of Gwynedd is something of a parallel to our own, then the languages would be similar. The French phrases sometimes creep in because there isn't any real English equivalent that wouldn't be awkward and draw the reader up short to say, "A-ha! She's tried to avoid the French phrase there, because there really isn't a France in the Eleven Kingdoms, but I know what she really wanted to say!"

   As for names, I've often grouped families of names from a particular region as a way of identifying them with the region that would be analogous to that place in our own world. For example, you find many of the Scottish names up in the north. The decidedly French ones tend to come from the southeast, which is close to where France would have been, if there were a France in the Eleven Kingdoms. Torenthi names tend to be either Moorish flavored or else have Polish and Slavonic roots—steppe influence. Obviously, this doesn't always work; and names do tend to migrate from their places of origin.

ELLIOT: The Deryni fantasies draw heavily on your background in medieval history, the kingdom of Gwynedd being roughly patterned after ninth century Wales. Why did you choose this specific era?

KURTZ: Wales actually provides only a part of the background for the Deryni series. When I wrote the first book, I had never been to Great Britain, and I had this intellectual fascination with Wales that was based solely on what I had read and intuited about that fantastic country. When, between the completion of *Deryni Rising* and *Deryni Checkmate*, I actually went to Wales, that fascination was confirmed; but I also went to Scotland for the first time, and the Yorkshire area—and those really turned me on. If there's such a thing as reincarnation, and I tend to think there is, then I've been in Scotland before. Crossing the border was almost a physical sensation; it was like coming home. Consequently, a lot more of Scottish and English flavor came into the later books, not just the Welsh influence. Living in Ireland hasn't had a great deal of direct impact on the imagery, but I recently visited Romania for the first time—just in time to incorporate some of that Eastern European and Orthodox flavor into my treatment of Torenth and other points east of Gwynedd.

As for time settings of the saga, I'm covering a two hundred year span just now, from around 916 to about 1125; and that's a period far enough removed in our own history that there's a great deal we don't know about it. That leaves me a lot of latitude in my speculations.

REGINALD: Is Gwynedd an offshoot of our own universe, or somehow a parallel world in which the geography and historical events have moved in a slightly different direction?

KURTZ: I think we're talking about the same thing, really. A divergence into a parallel is an offshoot, isn't it?

ELLIOT: What are some of the explicit and implicit assumptions which underlie the kingdom of Gwynedd?

KURTZ: The most explicit assumption is that magic works, though this has several aspects. We can define "magic" as any occurrence which seems to operate by means that we can't explain, especially if there seems to be no causal connection supported by scientific evidence. It's also been defined as science not yet understood, as it might be viewed by superstitious, non-scientific people. Much of what the Deryni do, much of what's considered magical by their contemporaries, is what we are beginning to call science today: telepathy, telekinesis, teleportation, healing. They use hypnosis, too, although they have the added advantage of forcing a receptive state, which we do not in this universe. Much of their so-called magical activity seems to take place within the trappings of what we might call "ceremonial magic," but there are things which are mystical, bordering on the religious. There are things which even they can't explain; they simply work "spells," and things happen.

Of course, modern psychologists would point out, and rightly so, that the purpose of ritual is to achieve a certain mental set, to get one into the right "head-space" to be able to turn the mind loose to realize special potentials which are not normally accessible at the conscious level. And this is true. But understanding how a phenomenon works doesn't make it any less valid. Whether the "spells" which the Deryni use are simply mnemonic devices to trigger certain mental sets, shorthand procedures for previously used rituals, is not important. What is important is that these are ways which work, for them, in gaining access to these higher human potentials. The fact that the Deryni discovered that these potentials can be awakened in some humans simply illustrates my belief that we all have some of these potentials, to some extent, and that if one works at it, one can always become better than one was.

In this, the Deryni are embarked upon the classic quest for the Philosopher's Stone, the aim of the ancient alchemists. These early researchers weren't really trying to make gold out of lead; they were trying to refine the human spirit and make it more valuable than it started out, to burn away the dross and reveal the perfected man. The Deryni are far from perfect, but they do understand the need for this constant quest for perfection, knowing that they can never *reach* it, but knowing also that if no one tries, no one will ever rise any higher than he is. They do the best they can with what they have been given. And a man's reach must exceed his grasp, else what's a Heaven for?

ELLIOT: How do you play God? How do you create an entire world?

KURTZ: Constructing an imaginary world is both easier and more difficult than the uninitiated might think. A lot depends on how large a story you have to tell, how far-ranging you're going to be in your storytelling—a lot of things. For a world that's going to show up in more than one book, one almost has to have a map. I have one, and I try to be very scrupulous about putting new places on it, as I use them in the stories. This is the only way to avoid geographic inconsistencies, and even that doesn't always work. I also keep genealogies, since so many of my characters are related in some way; I keep lists of members of different groups, with ages and physical descriptions and any distinctive features such as the color associated with their magic, if they're Deryni; drawings of ground plans of buildings where my characters spend a lot of time, especially if I plan for them to go back there again; coats of arms; places mentioned but not yet placed on the map; who's associated with what lands. I'd be lost if I didn't keep my lists.

    I also do timelines of events, as I've found out that's the only way for me to keep my interwoven plots and subplots from getting hopelessly tangled. The key to the whole thing is consistency; and this is something often muddled or missed by the neophyte. Whatever world one is writing about must be realized as a consistent whole.

REGINALD: You were kind enough to show me some of your unpublished notebooks, which are filled with genealogical charts, character notes, and the like. How have these background materials evolved as the series itself has grown?

KURTZ: Well, they've moved into larger binders, for a start. When one is working across a span of more than twenty years now, it would be impossible to keep all the relationships and character descriptions straight, without those notebooks. The form hasn't changed much over the years, and I still tend to jot down notes on scraps of paper, when new characters are developing. On days when I'm feeling organized, these end up in the notebooks. Even with all this background material, though, the occasional discrepancy creeps in. There's no way I could keep the details of twelve Deryni novels all in my head. (There's a parallel "bible" developing for the Adept series.)

REGINALD: How do you research a novel?

KURTZ: First, there's the obvious library and book research, to flesh out the original idea. That's mostly all one has to go on, for a fantasy project—though there are practical aspects, like knowledge of horses, costuming, castles, church ritual, and the like. Real world experience comes in here, too, like medical and law enforcement background, my training in hypnosis. I'm finding these particularly useful for the Adept series.

What's much more fun, though, is on-site research. This becomes especially important when one is working on a story with a real-world setting, like *Lammas Night* or the Adept books, though travel is certainly useful for ambience in fantasy novels. When I was writing *Lammas Night*, I visited all the locations that I used on the book. It was the first book I'd set in real history, and my first opportunity to make direct use of my training as a historian. More recently, in the Adept series, I've visited all the sites mentioned, driven all the roads. I "cased" Dunvegan Castle to figure out how my bad guys should break in to steal the Faery Flag—and sent a copy of the book to The MacLeod afterwards, so he'd be aware of the potential holes I'd spotted in his security arrangements. I drove the road from Skye to Loch Ness in a rainstorm—though we didn't jump the car from the ferry to the quay. I spent most of a day with the Lothian and Borders Police in Edinburgh, where my McLeod hangs out. I could go on and on.

The third kind of research is what I call the *practicum*—when you get right down to the nitty-gritty during the writing process, and sometimes try out what you're writing. I recall that when I was writing the scene in *Deryni Checkmate* where Morgan has been drugged with *merasha* and has fallen down the chute under St. Torin's shrine, and he's coming to—I got down on the floor and tried out that passage to see what he really would have seen as he regained consciousness. I did something similar to work out the scene in *High Deryni* where Declan Carmody had to grovel before the Regents. (Just how far onto the floor *does* one have to get, for a tormentor to easily put his boot on the back of one's neck?) Often, when I'm sitting at my word processor, I'm making the facial expressions and gestures of my characters as I'm writing the scene. All these kinds of research contribute to the background of any writing project.

ELLIOT: The Deryni universe is distinguished by your mastery of historical costuming. Have you created many such garments yourself?

KURTZ: I've always loved to wear costumes—and to make them. Perhaps this goes back to having fairy tales read to me as a child, before I could even understand what my mother was saying. I'm told that she read to me from the time I was an infant in arms, and that on my second birthday, I recited the entire poem of "Little Orphan Annie" for my grandparents. Around elementary school age, the boy across the street and I (and later, my younger sister) used to play knights and queen, and we rode stick horses with intricate harnesses, and carried cardboard shields. I remember a yellow cloak made out of an old chenille bedspread. Of course, Florida was too hot and humid to do much in the way of dressing up outside, at least in the daytime, but I'd draw pictures at night, and tell my friend to imagine that this was how we really looked.

But it wasn't until I came to California and discovered the Society for Creative Anachronism (SCA) that I really discovered the joys of historical costuming. I learned to sew when I was around seven or eight, and long ago reached the point where I'm not afraid to tackle much of anything, so far as a sewing project is concerned. (For example, I made my wedding gown, and learned many new sewing techniques in the process, such as sculptured lace appliqué.) Sewing medieval clothing is a little different, though, since you don't work with patterns in the usual sense. That took a little getting used to; and I've had my share of disasters, and done my share of ripping out. But making and wearing medievals, as we call them in the SCA, is still one of my favorite ways to unwind. And, of course, making and wearing these clothes teaches you a lot about what one could and could not do while wearing them, and the reasons for some of the design features.

These range from use intended for the garment, type of fabric available, *width* of fabric available—for you have to remember that in the very early medieval times, the size of the loom was limited, so when you had to hand-weave every piece of fabric, you were going to want to make optimum use of that piece, and you weren't going to want to cut it any more than necessary. Remember that the lady of the manor was responsible for clothing the entire household. She might have ladies to help her with the spinning and weaving and sewing, but this was pretty much a year-round occupation, just keeping clothing on everybody's back. When you have to go through that, you use and re-use every scrap of fabric, and cut down adult clothing for the children, and so on. We recycle clothes today, too.

ELLIOT: I note at least three major themes in your fantasy: first, there is nothing wrong with being different—different does not necessarily mean bad; second, power in itself is neither good nor evil; and third, one must not misuse the gifts one has been given, or rather, one has an obligation to use them as wisely as possible.

KURTZ: I think you've noted these threads in my fiction very well. The first one gets down to the basic notion of prejudice, I suppose. We encounter all kinds of prejudice today—racial, religious, ethnic, social class. The point is, prejudice is unfair. It isn't right to judge an individual on the basis of a group to which he belongs, especially if it's something over which he has no control. I suppose we could say that there are some areas of prejudice over which a person does have control, like religion or social class since, at least in theory, a person could change his religion or make a million dollars and bring himself up to a better social class. But things like skin color, or Deryniness—these can't very well be changed. Furthermore, it isn't right to expect that people should have to change. We should value the differences in people.

As for the second theme, the amoral nature of power, it's the use of power which takes on moral coloring. Atomic energy is an obvious modern example; the bomb versus nuclear medicine. Or, to shade the judgment a little, a reactor which goes critical—power intended for good but gone astray—versus a well-run nuclear generator which benignly produces energy to power a whole state. Getting into the more human resources, we might use the example of a brilliant scientist doing research in bacteriology. He can look for a cure for cancer, or he can develop items for bacteriological warfare. The same genius, but turned to different ends. Among the Deryni, the contrasts are even more obvious, some of them using their enormous power to protect, some to destroy, some to heal, some to subvert the weak. Wencit of Torenth, for example, without his drive to regain what he felt was his by whatever means possible, might have turned out quite differently. There was enormous power and potential there, yet he ended up destroyed—and it had to be that way.

Finally, there is the theme of using one's gifts wisely. I think this is a definite area which carries over into our lives. Everyone has various potentials, but they have to be realized. First, one has to recognize he or she has got these potentials, and then one has to develop them. Cinhil is probably the best example in the books. He fights like hell to avoid doing and being what he was born to do and be. The problem with Cinhil is that he was born to do and be several things, and the society in which he lives can't handle him doing both. He's led a peaceful and fulfilling religious life for most of his years when we first encounter him. He's a good priest and quite contemplative. He could have spent the rest of his life behind the cloister walls and been perfectly content. He probably would have made a positive contribution to the life of his religious community, too. But he's also a prince of the royal blood, the only one left. And there comes the time when the need for him in this other, secular role, is greater than the need for him to stay in his monastery. You'll recall that poignant conversation he has with Archbishop Anscom, the night he's to be married to Megan, in which the Archbishop points out the new duties which call. And Cinhil knows that Anscom is right, at least in his head. But he never manages to convince his heart, and that plagues him for the rest of his life, though he does attain a measure of personal fulfillment once he resumes his priestly offices in private— especially once he confides in Alister-Camber and has someone with whom to share this aspect of his life.

REGINALD: But you've also increasingly emphasized in your most recent novels the need to address a higher moral authority, and have given much more attention both to religious and Deryni ceremony. Some critics have said that the overuse of such elements make the Heirs of Saint Camber Trilogy "ponderous and slow-moving," although I personally have found these novels the most moving and character-centered of all your fiction, perhaps because they are tragedies. How do you respond to such gibes?

KURTZ: The obvious rejoinder is that one can't please everyone. The ceremonies, both religious and Deryni, are there for good reasons, to advance both the plots and the development of the characters. Many modern readers are reluctant to let themselves become emotionally involved with issues that go beyond the superficial, and they tend to be especially uncomfortable dealing with moral or spiritual issues. There's nothing I can do about that other than to offer my interpretations of such themes via my characters and stories, and hope that the work resonates for a large segment of the rest of my readers. But I'd remind critics that tragedies do require a heavier touch than lighter tale-telling. Without making any value judgment, I'm not a Terry Pratchett or a Robert Asprin, much though I admire their work within its own genre.

ELLIOT: You've written extensively on the genetics of Deryni inheritance.

KURTZ: In some respects, I've written far more extensively than I should have done. Some of my speculations have come back to haunt me. I've had to revise my theories more than once, but they were always that: theories.

The notes on genetic aspects of Deryni inheritance were a first crack at figuring out how the Haldane potential is transmitted. Initially, I postulated it being carried on the Y chromosome, which would endow all males of the line with the capability to have Deryni-like abilities put to them. In theory, this would mean there's no reason why all Haldanes couldn't assume Deryni powers—except that Haldanes have always been given the impression that only the King can hold the power at any one time. We know now that isn't true—Tiercel de Claron never believed it, and proved it wasn't so, in his work with Conall—but it undoubtedly was a useful fiction in the beginning, to prevent multiple Haldanes from acquiring Deryni-like powers and then endangering the succession by squabbling among themselves. Javan may have suspected, very early on, for he experienced the spontaneous awakening of many of his powers, perhaps catalyzed by regular contact with the powerful Deryni Tavis O'Neill; but his former regents managed to eliminate him before he got a chance to explore the possibility. He did know that his brother Rhys Michael was developing shields.

Two centuries later, it's probable that Kelson and his mentors are on the brink of making the connection. After all, they were able to partially empower Nigel, to safeguard the succession before heading off on a military campaign in which Kelson might be killed. Once Kelson has an heir of his own, will he attempt to reverse this? As far as guarding the rightful succession, there's no chance of Nigel trying to usurp his nephew's throne—not Nigel, that most *parfait* knight. But if Nigel retains what he has been given, and perhaps continues to develop Deryni-like abilities, Kelson and has mentors may well have to revise their acceptance of what has always been taught.

And if all or most Haldanes receive Deryni powers, is it likely that the potential is unique to Haldanes? The answer has to be no, because we've already seen notable examples of "humans" being at least partially empowered, in the persons of Ian Howell and Bran Coris. We also know that some Deryni, like Tavis and Sylvan, can "block" powers in other Deryni.

All of the above suggests that perhaps those individuals who have powers triggered in them were actually some sort of Deryni all along, who either have of on-off switch tripped during the ritual process. What if the Haldane potential, the predisposition to receive Deryni empowerment, is actually a very small sub-set of the general Deryni pool, similar to the sub-set of Healers who have the ability to block Deryni powers? Perhaps such individuals are born "blocked" and remain that way until something catalyzes them. Obviously, the entire Deryni genetic question is far more complicated than I'd first imagined.

I suspect that the factors involved are more like the ones that determine eye color, for example—multiple factors that can combine in different ways with different results. And, of course, even inherited Deryniness is only a potential in the sense that born Deryni still have to be trained, to realize their abilities. Otherwise, you get people like old Bethane, who learn just enough to be dangerous.

Incidentally, the old Y chromosome theory doesn't at all address the question of Haldane princesses possibly carrying the potential. Other than Nigel's infant daughter, we haven't seen any Haldane princesses of the blood, but they certainly exist; I've simply left them off the genealogical charts for purposes of clarity. As the old adage goes, absence of proof is not proof of absence.

ELLIOT: How do you maintain logic and consistency in a series which now comprises twelve novels and a collection of short stories, and must number in the millions of published words?

KURTZ: It isn't easy, and it gets harder as the years go by and the universe expands. A lot depends on how large your concept is for the universe you're developing. Authors who set out to write one book, with no thoughts of continuing in that universe, tend to write themselves into corners and out of the possibilities of sequels. If they later decide to do a sequel, they may have a rough time of it. *Dune Messiah* is a good example of this. Frank Herbert wrote a monumental masterpiece in *Dune*, but he wasn't thinking in terms of a sequel. By the time he went on to do *Dune Messiah*, he had a lot of corners to write himself out of, and the book suffers as a result. But he planned ahead for *Children of Dune*, and that book, while not as good as *Dune*, was infinitely better than *Dune Messiah*. Then there are authors who drive their readers crazy by not worrying whether every little detail is consistent from book to book, as long as each book is consistent within itself. Marion Zimmer Bradley, who is one of my very favorite people, does this a bit in her Darkover books, and it's certainly understandable, considering the vast time span over which she's written the books. Some of the inconsistencies she merely shrugs off. There's one, however, that I love, where she explains away a differing account by saying that this particular character was under a great deal of stress at the time a specific incident occurred, and he may not have remembered exactly how it happened, that his memory may have been mercifully blurred. It takes a rare and special talent to pull off that kind of escape from inconsistency, and Marion is an expert. Now that I'm more than twenty years into the Deryni series, I only hope I can resolve inconsistencies as gracefully.

ELLIOT: The meticulous attention to detail in the Deryni books has prompted comments from readers that these novels read just like history, and this would certainly fit with your educational background. Is there a danger of loading the reader down with too much detail?

KURTZ: I don't think my attention to detail is so much a product of my historical background as it is just a part of me. I'm a very visual person. I have a vivid imagination, especially for scenes and colors and sounds. Some people have commented that the opening of *Deryni Rising* reads as though written for the screen—which is interesting, since I did at one point write a film version of that book (it wasn't produced, alas). I didn't necessarily have that in mind when I wrote it, though. That's just the way it came out. If anything, it's the result of the scientific observation that I was taught before I ever entertained the idea of being either a historian or a writer.

Certainly, it's possible to go into too much detail. But it's not so much how *much* you tell as *how* you tell it that makes the difference. A good description, if it's properly balanced with action and dialogue, can be a great asset to creating the proper atmosphere in a story. If it's overdone, it can drag the whole thing down. Oddly enough, I've been criticized both for too much and not enough description. I suspect that the too-much advocates are the ones who are not strong visualizers themselves—and there's nothing wrong with that—and they really *do* get bogged down with so much detail that they just can't envision the scene in their minds' eyes.

Early on, about the time I was starting the Camber books, Lester del Rey called me on omitting some of that detail. As I recall, I'd talked about setting Wards Major many times in the course of several books, and tried a shorthand description of what happens in the process. Lester came back and said, "Katherine, you have to remember that some of your readers are picking up any given book for the first time, and they may not have read the expanded version of what is old-hat to you by now. Besides, they love your magic. They want it in all its details. So don't short-change them." He's right, of course. The trick is to retell those things that have become familiar to me, in ways that are fresh and won't bore me or my faithful readers, yet will still give that first-time excitement to the reader who is encountering it for the first time. But I'm not sure how many more ways I can describe setting wards with ward cubes.

REGINALD: In the process of editing the books, have pieces been cut out to smooth the narrative flow?

KURTZ: Canny editors have cut the occasional superfluous word or phrase, but rarely anything much bigger. My interweaving of plots and sub-plots is usually too tight to permit excising very much without causing a ripple effect all through the rest of the book. And I do write long. *King Javan's Year* came in at 765 manuscript pages, well over a hundred pages longer than they'd been expecting for budgeting purposes; but the editors at Del Rey Books couldn't find anywhere to make serious cuts without doing serious damage to the story—so it's been published in its entirety, slightly thicker and priced slightly higher than originally planned. I *have* promised not to get so carried away in the future.

ELLIOT: Where did the Deryni come from?

KURTZ: The original idea for the series—or should I say, the idea which later led to the Deryni concept—came from a dream I had back in 1965. That was just the ghost of the story later told in *Deryni Rising*. Jehana was the one who had to assume the dead King's power, and Kelson was an infant in arms. There was also the possibility of a romantic interest between Morgan and Jehana. "Lords of Sorandor" was reprinted in *The Deryni Archives*. It was that story which I described to Stephen Whitfield, in an expanded version. Reading that story today, it's interesting to see what parts got translated almost intact in the final novel, and what things changed radically.

I can't tell you where the Deryni themselves came from. They weren't in "Lords of Sorandor," at least by name. I wish I could remember how I discovered them, but it's been too long, and I've been too intimately involved with them for too long, to be able to recapture that discovery process. It is really more of a discovery process than a creative one, by the way. My readers have remarked, but not before I'd realized it myself, that at times, it's as though I'm recounting real history, not just telling a story I've made up. It's enough to make one wonder if it isn't possible, perhaps, to tap into another dimension. Maybe there really *are* Deryni, somewhere, somewhen. When one of those characters takes a storyline and runs, it certainly seems like there's something at work besides mere imagination.

REGINALD: But were the Deryni always present in the Eleven Kingdoms, or are they of relatively recent historical origin?

KURTZ: I don't think the Deryni were always there, but I'm not yet sure just when they appeared. This may well emerge when I do the books dealing with the consolidation of Gwynedd under Augarin Haldane.

ELLIOT: Many avid readers of fantasy have stated that the strong lead characters (male and female) in your work are particularly attractive and memorable when compared with their counterparts in other contemporary SF.

KURTZ: I suppose the major difference between my characters and a lot of other fantasy characters is that mine are full of very human foibles and faults, even the heroes. By the time you've gotten to know a Morgan or a Duncan, you know a lot about what makes them tick. They're complex. The heroes aren't all white, the villains aren't all black. I'd say that the ones my readers identify most closely with are Morgan, of course, Duncan, Derry (which was something of a surprise to me, since he started out as a very minor character), Rhys, Evaine, and Camber. I feel closest to Camber myself, with Duncan probably a close second. In many respects Camber is sort of a Deryni Thomas More with a lot of added attractions. He's an extremely ethical man who has to deal with situation-ethics a great deal of the time, and it bothers him, even though he really believes he's doing the right things for the right reasons.

Cinhil is another character that I feel I know very well, though I don't like a lot of the things about him. He goes a long way, from the time we first see him living in his monastery, until he dies in *Camber the Heretic*. So does Camber, for that matter. Camber is very real for me. I'd know him if I ran into him on the street. (I should. He's peered over my shoulder at the typewriter or word processor often enough!) I'm very fond of Rhys, too, though I don't understand what makes him tick as well as I do Camber. And Evaine is like me in many respects, especially her passion for learning about things and solving puzzles.

ELLIOT: Speaking of your characters, how did you go about selecting their names?

KURTZ: I collect names. Whenever I go to a foreign country, I look for books on "What to Name Your Baby." I have them from England, Wales, Scotland, Cornwall, and Ireland, to name but a few. I like the Celtic flavor, and I like formal-sounding names. I hate nicknames, for the most part, especially the diminutives—Bobby, Johnny, Billy, Tommy. Yuck! The fastest way I know of to get my fur bristled the wrong way is to call me Kathy. So many people think they're indicating friendliness by calling a person by a nickname, even when they've been introduced by a given name. When I introduce myself as Katherine Kurtz, it's because I think of myself as Katherine, and I want to be called that. If I wanted to be called Kathy, I'd introduce myself that way. That's one of my few pet peeves. I always call someone by the name they want to be called.

Names are very important. I would never name a child of mine a name that could be corrupted by unthinking clods—at least not a name that could have a diminutive ending put on it. My little nephew's name is Graham, for example. No way you're going to put a "y" ending on that and have it sound like a cutesy name. And I have a half-sister named Brenda. Again, no way to shorten that badly. As for my characters' names, I use historical names and made-up ones. I'll often use a less common spelling, like Brion. Occasionally, a character will address another by a shortened form, such as Alister addressing Jebediah as Jeb in a casual situation—but not a diminutive!

REGINALD: There seems to be a curious dichotomy in your selection of names for the royal house of Haldane, however. The naming patterns here appear to be at variance with those of real-life medieval monarchies, where repetition of names, particularly of the better-known members of each family, was the common practice.

KURTZ: I'm aware of this anomaly. When writing fiction, however, it can be confusing to the reader to have too many characters with the same name, or even names that are too similar. I've had the Haldanes repeat some of the traditional family names as secondary names, but I've tried to keep the regnal names fairly distinct, for the sake of clarity. The way I weave plots, it's the least I can do for my readers, who are already struggling to keep all the characters straight. Even *I* can't keep them straight all of the time. (Did you really think I started including the Indices of Characters and Places just for the edification of my readers?)

ELLIOT: Most science fiction and fantasy writers avoid religion in their work, or at the least gloss it over. Yet the Deryni books draw extensively on religious themes, customs, myths, and ceremonies.

KURTZ: It isn't particularly surprising to me that other writers tend to avoid this topic in their stories. I think the modern trend is to feel that religion is increasingly unimportant in the light of scientific sophistication. People brought up in a technological age, especially those with a strong scientific education, tend to distrust anything they can't see or measure. They view religion as the opiate of the masses, a psychological crutch which the progressed man doesn't need anymore. They think that organized religion, with its myths and customs and ceremonies, is out of date in these modern times. And if it's out of date now, it will surely be out of date in the future. Hence, when you encounter religion as a salient point in most science fiction, it's in the context of either a decadent civilization or a primitive planet where the progressive Earthmen are going to release the natives from theocratic bondage. Perhaps this is a harsh judgment, and there are exceptions to this generalization, but this is my impression.

Even when most science fiction writers do try to deal with religion in a meaningful way, they come up short because they try to invent an alien religion without realizing what religion is all about. The result is that the religions *do* come out as shallow and unsophisticated, thereby proving the writers' theories that religion is an unimportant appendage of human psychology, and not worthy of the sophisticated and educated modern man. Fortunately, some science fiction writers do eventually reach the point of some of their really advanced scientist brothers and sisters, who have discovered that, in the long run, that they *have* to acknowledge some universal Creative Force, Something to account for the majesty and order of the universe. This is basically a return to the foundation of religion, albeit in a more nebulous, less formal manner.

Unfortunately, when most people reach this point, when they've experienced the Great Awe, they become inarticulate about it. Theologians will write about it, but scientists generally don't. That's a shame, because I think they could give us some beautiful insights from their unique point of view. I *am* surprised, though, that more fantasy writers don't deal with religion, since they tend to have a liberal (as opposed to a hard science) education, and should have been exposed to human history in greater depth than one would expect of a scientist. Given a historical orientation, it's almost impossible not to realize that the Church in the Middle Ages, especially, was the single most overpowering influence that touched the life of every man, woman, and child, even more than kings and warriors. Since most fantasy writers draw heavily on a medieval or quasi-medieval background, it's amazing that so many of them ignore this important point.

Again, perhaps it's because they're uncomfortable talking about something which is really so close to the human center, whether you're talking about Judeo-Christian religion or the gentler aspects of the Old Religions. Modern man doesn't often have time to seek a mystical experience, and I think this is reflected in what is being written today, not just in fantasy and science fiction, but in all kinds of literature. Drug culture used this quest for the mystical as an excuse for their activities, but drugs have a tendency to become the end rather than the means. Some people are discovering that a mind-high is much better than a drug-high, and with no nasty side-effects; but achieving this state only with your own head takes a lot more discipline and control than just popping a pill or lighting up a joint or shooting up something.

I don't take drugs, I don't even like to take an aspirin unless it's really necessary. But I've had some experiences that were absolutely mind-boggling. The mystical experience is something that still gives me shivers of sheer awe. I suppose I've drawn a little on that in the Camber books, especially. Remember, I told you that there was a lot of me in Camber. I've used this religious approach in the Deryni books both because of the historical framework, and because I guess I want to try to share a little of the magic of what religious experience can be. If you put that kind of thing in a fantasy novel, people who ordinarily would be a little skittish about acknowledging this part of them, in their modern, scientific educations, are often able to taste it just a little. And some of them go on and explore further on their own.

Religion can be the opiate of the masses, as some folks charge, but if you take it a few steps beyond dogma and get to the archetypal foundations, the mystery of existence, you can find something that is valid and has meaning, at different levels for different people. The outward form isn't that important. Personally, I'm most comfortable in a Judeo-Christian framework similar to what I describe in the books, but I can also be comfortable in any of a number of other frameworks. People may call their gods by different names, and acknowledge Him or Her in different ways, but it all goes back to the Source, in the end. There are many different paths to the Godhead.

ELLIOT: Has the Deryni series bridged the gap between SF fans and the mainstream?

KURTZ: I think it has, to a certain extent. I've had reports that people who never read fantasy before have picked up my books and gotten hooked on them, and then started branching out to other fantasy and science fiction. People who like straight historical fiction also like the books. They've also been great for getting junior high and high school kids to start reading—kids who've never read a whole book before in their lives. I've had some amazing reports from teachers who use the books as catalysts for getting kids to read. I do plan to do other things besides the Deryni, though. I mentioned the book on the medieval sheriff. I also have a couple of mainstream projects currently underway.

ELLIOT: Some critics have said that the early Deryni books are not as deftly written as the later ones. Would you agree?

KURTZ: Of course I would. I wrote *Deryni Rising* in 1969; I was decades younger and less experienced then. Also, this is a much simpler book, in terms of plot and characters, than any of the later ones. People don't usually realize, until I point it out to them, that *Deryni Rising* takes place in little more than twenty-four hours, other than the first chapter. There's just so much you can do in that time frame, especially if it's a first novel and you're still finding your literary balance. If I were writing the book today, there are some things I'd add, and if a film version eventually comes out, folks will see additional material there. It doesn't change the basic story, but the script I wrote some years ago is much more the way the story would have gone if I'd written it today. It's a bit expanded, and shows a little more of the relationship between Morgan and Brion and Kelson. We actually see Morgan before he goes off to Cardosa, and a little of his relationship with Kelson. It's great fun.

As for progress, I would certainly hope that the later books are better ones. If they aren't, it means that I haven't been learning my lessons as an author. I'm told, for example, that *The Harrowing of Gwynedd* is the best one to date, and I have to agree. I like that book very much. I still re-read passages from time to time and think to myself, "Wow, that's neat. Did I really write that?" And the neatest part of all is that I did! If I didn't enjoy writing so much, I wouldn't do it. It's nice that other people like to read what I've written, but if it didn't please me, too, I certainly wouldn't spend all those hours behind the word processor.

REGINALD: Your work has also gotten more serious as the Deryni series has progressed.

KURTZ: Certainly, the themes treated in the Camber sequence are more serious—and in the Heirs of St. Camber books, which are really direct sequels to *Camber the Heretic*. It was a dark time in the history of Gwynedd, and terrible sacrifices were made by many good people. The story needed to be told, because the prospect of genocide is not that far removed from our own experience in this century; ethnic cleansing is just a step further down the lane from the Final Solution. My most difficult task in this regard has been threading enough courage and hope through the stories that the reader isn't left feeling utterly depressed. Good may not always succeed in the short term, but Evil will never gain the final victory if enough good men and women do something.

I've dealt with serious issues in the King Kelson Trilogy, too, but there's also a lighter touch, by having Dhugal as a foil for Kelson. And when I do the book in which Kelson finally gets to keep a worthy bride—hopefully within the next few years—we'll have a happy ending for a change.

ELLIOT: Your characters speak with a decidedly modern cant.

KURTZ: Language seems to be the thing that's criticized most by reviewers. They seem to think that fantasy has to be full of thee's and thou's and lots of archaic language. That can be good, if it's done well, but it can make a book limp along very badly if it isn't just right. I'm not J. R. R. Tolkien or C. S. Lewis, and I don't think it's valid to criticize the Deryni books because my language is not theirs. I try to keep blatant modernisms out of the language, but I *am* writing for modern readers, and communication is sometimes more important than formal style. There are those who can handle epic language beautifully, and I admire them for it, but I don't think that the stories I have to tell would benefit from being couched in that form.

Mary Stewart's Merlin books are beautiful examples of language handling. And there's a novel called *The White Hart* by Nancy Springer that's marvelous. But I don't think either of these ladies could tell the Deryni stories as well as I can. Different kinds of tales call for different ways of telling. Still, I am aware of the fact that my language usage bothers some folks, and I'm trying to broaden the epic sweep of what I'm doing.

ELLIOT: Lester del Rey, retired editor of the Del Rey fantasy series, has been criticized by some historians of the field for his "crass commercial motives." You've said: "I admire and respect him tremendously. I couldn't ask for a better mentor at this stage of my career."

KURTZ: I enjoyed working with him while he was editor of the fantasy line at Ballantine Books, and felt that I learned a great deal from him. I read a lot of his work during my formative years, and it was very satisfying to work with him as I built my place in the genre. His instincts about the Deryni were very good, for the most part, and the few disagreements we had were always resolved to the betterment of the books, and in a manner which was not personally negative for either of us. We still like and respect each other. I can't imagine why there's such a wide divergence of opinion about him.

REGINALD: Have you become better at editing your own work as the years (and books) have progressed?

KURTZ: I think one's instincts certainly improve with experience. In general, I've gotten better. Something of a down-side has been changing from a typewriter to a word processor. While it's an undeniable time saver—and I would never even consider going back to the typewriter—the sheer ease with which one can make changes tends to encourage overwriting. (I think this is a serious impediment that upcoming new writers are having to face. I can usually tell, within the first dozen pages, whether an aspiring author's story has been written on a computer; the tendency is not to tighten but to expand, all too often to the point of redundancy.)

One can eliminate some or even most of this tendency by printing out hard copy as an interim stage, and being brutal with a red pen—and I do this. And, of course, one saves several weeks per book, just not having to retype that final draft. Computers are wonderful servants, so long as they don't insinuate themselves to the point that their technology becomes master.

ELLIOT: Of your fans, you state: "They have been very good to me, and have rewarded my attention to them with astonishing loyalty and devotion."

KURTZ: Fans provide an author with positive feedback on his or her work. They also provide an interaction that isn't possible while the author is actually sitting behind the typewriter or computer. This is important, especially when one occasionally runs into glitches and needs reassurances. Fans also give one different perspectives which sometimes lead to new ideas. One of the things I've done is to work with a couple of Illinois fans to produce a Deryni magazine. I hesitate to call it a fanzine, since it's really more of a journal on things Deryni, and it's a bit higher caliber than the average fanzine.

It's called *Deryni Archives: The Magazine*, and I think one of its most important functions is that it helps span the gap between books. Fans can get very anxious and impatient when they have to wait one-to-two years between books, but since that's the best I've been able to do so far, the *Deryni Archives* provides a showcase for their efforts and a way for me to keep them abreast of the latest developments and my current plans. It does take a bit of time that some could argue might be better spent actually working on more books, but there's got to be a balance, for the readers' sakes. Fan mail is another direct vehicle of communication between an author and his or her public. I get a fair amount, some of it forwarded through Ballantine, and some of it sent direct, and so far, I've managed to answer all of it personally. It may take a while, at times, but I think it's important if a fan takes the time and effort to write, that the author makes some kind of response. It's dismal to send off those letters and just have them vanish in the abyss. I don't know how long I'll be able to keep up the personal letter answering, but I'm certainly going to try to keep some line of communication open.

ELLIOT: For many years, you were an officer and member of the Society for Creative Anachronism.

KURTZ: The Society for Creative Anachronism is an educational, non-profit corporation whose function is to re-create the positive aspects of the Middle Ages as they existed in Western Europe. They put on tournaments and feasts and revels, study the various art forms—calligraphy, illumination, music, dance, costuming—and practice them. There are branches in nearly every part of the country, and some outside the continental United States. Part of the idea of the SCA is tied in with the concept called "living history," in which one learns by doing. Most of what I know about medieval fighting techniques, for example, has been learned from watching it in an SCA context. I wrote ceremonies for the SCA, gleaned from historical research—and then got to see them actually done by real people. Hence, a lot of the pageantry I write about in the books, I've seen and helped stage in the SCA. This is very valuable.

When I dedicated *Camber of Culdi* partly to the "good folk of the Society for Creative Anachronism, without whom this book would have been finished far sooner but far less well," I wasn't kidding. I spent a lot of time with the SCA, but I have also gotten a lot out of it. It was a good investment. I've been the equivalent of a Prime Minister or Chancellor; I've been a reigning Princess and Queen; I've been a Herald. I've known the awfulness of watching my champion slain in the lists—and of seeing him win me a crown. I've made and worn clothing of the period. I've cooked medieval meals and produced calligraphed and illuminated scrolls, done galliards and montards and bransles and pavanes and Scottish dances. I've also seen the real devotion of modern-day knights to their vows of chivalry, helped them plan vigils the night before they were to receive the knightly accolade, sat on a grim Court of Chivalry called to chastise a knight who had not lived up to his vows in the SCA contest. I've also made medieval bardings for my horse and tilted at rings and the quintain, though I've never jousted at a human opponent. (The SPCA doesn't approve, and the horses aren't crazy about it either). All of these experiences enriched my existence and made me better able to write about these things.

ELLIOT: Asked about the chief differences between male and female fantasy writers, you contend that the best fantasy today is being written by women.

KURTZ: I can't explain why, but it's simply been my observation that this is largely true, at least for the kind of fantasy I like to read. One can start with Anne McCaffrey and Andre Norton, go on with Patricia McKillip and Tanith Lee and C. J. Cherryh and Marion Zimmer Bradley, and wind up with a newer writer like Mercedes Lackey. Some of these women also write science fiction, or mix science fiction and fantasy, but their common point is that they all write good fantasy. I should also mention Mary Stewart and Evangeline Walton, of course, and I've undoubtedly left out some important ones, particularly among the younger group.

I think, perhaps, that women tend to be more intuitive, as opposed to being hard-science oriented—more concerned with people rather than things and events, and perhaps it's this which gives us a slight edge in writing the kind of fantasy I enjoy. Notice that I qualify good fantasy as the kind *I* enjoy, which is entirely subjective. But that's what counts in reading tastes, in the long run. Sometimes one can tell why one likes a particular work; sometimes one can't—but one can almost always say whether one likes or doesn't like it. It's greatly a matter of personal taste. Not that I don't like and admire some of my male colleagues, like Poul Anderson—far from it. But some of the things most hyped in the past have been things I've enjoyed the least—and they have tended to be written by men. I can't explain the correlation.

ELLIOT: What plans do you have for the future?

KURTZ: I have at least another six to eight books to do in the Deryni series, though I expect to do some other things along the way, too. And if more ideas come along for more Deryni books, I'll do them too, as long as I continue to enjoy them. In addition to the three-book sequence on Morgan's childhood and origins (the Childe Morgan Trilogy), and the current trilogy, The Heirs of Saint Camber (*King Javan's Year*, the second book, was just published, and *The Captive Kings*, the concluding volume, is almost finished), I'd like to do a book about Kelson falling in love and finding a permanent relationship (yes, he does finally marry!). I think that could be a very interesting project, and one which I know that a large number of my readers are interested in. There are all kinds of possibilities.

I don't see any definite end to the series—partly because that would mean a cessation of the creative processes. When you create a whole world, if you've created it in multiple dimensions, you can't help but have it continue to generate more stories. There's always the question cropping up of, "What happened then?" Or, "What happened before that?" Or, "What about so-and-so?" The concepts and characters will vary, and the way I look at them, as I grow in my awareness and in my skill at transmitting that awareness to my readers; but the possibilities are extensive. I see other, non-Deryni products on the horizon, and perhaps they will eventually take precedence over the Deryni, but if they do, it will only be because I have grown into other areas of concern, and have other tales to tell, and other lessons to teach, and other wonders to discover.

The Adept books are a step in that direction; Book IV is currently under contract, to go hardcover in 1994, and I already have the plotline for Book V firmly in mind. In 1993/94, I'll also be doing a major book for Bantam Books set during the American War for Independence—*Two Crowns for America*, a tale of Freemasonry, Jacobite Intrigue, and American Crypto-History. I'm also contracted for another book for Bantam, but haven't yet decided what that will be. I'm looking forward to figuring it out.

REGINALD: You mentioned the Adept series, the new sequence of occult detective novels appearing from Ace Books. In what sense are these true collaborations with Deborah Turner Harris?

KURTZ: Unlike many collaborations these days, I've had a major ongoing hand in the Adept books since the beginning. (I look upon Adam Sinclair as a sort of spiritual successor to Dion Fortune's Docter Taverner—a project I'd been wanting to get around to for years, but my contract commitments were else-where.) The original mandate offered was that I should conceptualize and out-line the books; then I was to choose a junior writing partner who was published but not yet well known, and he/she would "prose" it, or write a polished first draft—after which I would edit and polish and/or rewrite where necessary. This would give me the advantage of doing a long-postponed project sooner than it would have gotten done solo, and with less time investment; and it would give the junior author the advantage of working with a more established writer and gaining the name recognition of being linked with that person. In the instance of Deborah Turner Harris, our working relationship soon developed all the most positive aspects of a classic apprentice situation.

As it happens, Betty Ballantine had made a point of introducing Debby and me at the Worldcon in Brighton. (Betty had bought my first three books twenty years ago, while she was still at Ballantine, and she had bought Debby's first three, about fifteen years later, and thought we should know one another.) In the next few years, I had read all three of Debby's so-far published novels, and liked what I had read; and since she lives in St. Andrews with her Scottish hus-band (and my husband and I spend a lot of time in Scotland), we had a chance to pursue the friendship in person as well as by letter and phone and occasional professional encounters, such as the World Fantasy Convention in London.

So when I was approached to do a collaborative project for Ace, Deborah Turner Harris was my first and really only choice. I felt that our styles were complimentary enough to mesh well—I'd remarked at the time I read her first novel that I would love to see her characters sit down at table with Camber and his family, and eavesdrop on their conversation—and even more important, I was confident that we could work well together on a long-term project, both by personal and professional compatibility and by physical logistics.

The project has been a true collaboration from the very start, and both suc-cessful and enjoyable beyond either of our wildest dreams. Once I've solidified the outline for a book (anything from 60 to 100 pages in length—the more detail I can give her up front, the less work for both of us down the line), we meet several times to discuss what's going to happen. When possible, we both visit all the sites that will figure in the book; one or the other of us has always done so. Then Debby starts prosing the outline, sending me 4-5 chapter installments on floppy disk at 6-8 week intervals. While I'm polishing what she's sent, she's working on the next installment. When I finish my installment, I send back a floppy with the changed section, so she can see what I've done, and usually have 4-6 weeks to work on the current Deryni project while she's finishing the next installment. (She gets her break to work on *her* solo projects while I'm putting the final touches on the finished manuscript and then shifting my energies to work out the next outline.)

At this writing, we've just started on Adept IV, and I have V and most of VI firmly in mind for the future. We've decided that we very much like work-ing together this way, each alternating our partnership efforts with our solo projects, and we plan to continue as long as there's a demand for the series and I keep coming up with ideas.

I'd like to add here that the apprenticeship aspect has paid off very well already. Partly on the strength of her performance in the Adept series, Debby recently sold the first book of a new fantasy series to Ace, with an option to take at least two more—and they've already exercised the option. The first book of her new Calidon series will be out in 1993—but she'll be doing Adept IV before she starts on Calidon II.

REGINALD: If you could pick an epitaph for yourself, what would it be?

KURTZ: This is really difficult. Maybe something like:

KATHERINE KURTZ
Story-Teller and Catalyst
In Lightening the Hours for Her Readers
She Also Opened Their Minds
To the Infinite Potentials
Of the Human Spirit

REGINALD: Amen.

AFTERWORD

Imaginary History:
A Genealogical Approach

BY KATHERINE KURTZ

Whether one is aiming for a vision of the far future, the far past, or a place-time that never was/will be, a well-structured view of the general historical setting of the story enhances it—and ill attention to this facet of story-telling can ruin the otherwise best-crafted of tales. In any science fiction or fantasy tale which attempts to evoke a sense of historicity, a consistent and logical historical plan is essential.

I've found that one of the most interesting and useful forms of laying out history for me and the type of fiction I write is through the use of genealogical charts. While these need not ever see the light of anywhere besides the author's own study or office—and I stress that I see these as tools, not ends in themselves; the reader of the finished story may know nothing of their existence—properly structured charts of this kind can not only help to keep characters and their relationships sorted out, but they can actually suggest story turns that were never consciously intended at the time one put the charts together.

It still amazes me when such connections suddenly become apparent, in one of those blinding "Eureka!" experiences; and I haven't yet decided whether my unconscious is simply craftier than I give it credit for, laying in extra information at several levels of consciousness when I'm constructing such charts, or whether the information somehow filters through from elsewhere/when in some seemingly magical way—a suspicion which my scientifically-trained brain/mind rejects, but which the more intuitive mind/soul side of me increasingly tends to entertain, the more I watch some of my characters take off and "do their own thing," at times even telling *me* about their history.

Whatever the explanation, it happens; and this business of developing histories through genealogies is a fascinating one. A case in point is the development of the lineage of the Haldane Kings in the Deryni series.

It all began at the end of *High Deryni*, when I thought it would be a good idea to give at least a partial timeline of basic events surrounding the Festillic Interregnum, the bare chronology of Camber's life, and the events immediately preceding the events of the Deryni Trilogy. A listing of the Post-Interregnum Kings of Gwynedd seemed like a simple place to begin. What appeared in the appendices of *High Deryni* looked something like this, with the dates being indicative of reigns, not life spans:

117

Cinhil	904-917 (13 years)
Alroy	917-921 (4 years)
Javan	921-922 (1 year)
Rhys	922-928 (6 years)
Owain	928-948 (20 years)
Uthyr	948-980 (32 years)
Nygel	980-983 (3 years)
Jasher	983-985 (2 years)
Cluim	985-994 (9 years)
Urien	994-1025 (31 years)
Malcolm	1025-1074 (49 years)
Donal	1074-1095 (21 years)
Brion	1095-1120 (25 years)
Kelson	1120-

I must confess that at the time I put this together, I simply took the time span between Camber and Kelson which I had already established, wrote down a list of noble-sounding names, and filled in what seemed like logical time-spans for reigns.

I knew very little about the Haldane line before Brion, other than the vague realization that the line from Malcolm through Kelson was from father to son in all cases—that is, no brothers inherited. I also knew that Cinhil, one of the younger sons of a very large family, had been the only Haldane to survive the Festillic Coup. I also reasoned that since Cinhil had been a forty-four-year-old monk just before he came to the throne, his heirs after a thirteen-year reign would have to have been minor sons—which implies a regency for at least a time, and would account for some of the turmoil surrounding the infamous Council of Ramos and the great persecutions which plagued the Deryni two centuries before the time of King Kelson. And that was enough for the end of *High Deryni*.

However, when I began working on *Camber of Culdi*, it soon became apparent that I needed to map out Cinhil's end of the line in greater detail. I started at the other end, however, since I figured that charting out the Haldane relationships that I already *knew* would get me started on the right track for Cinhil's end of things. And so the later Haldanes worked out like that shown in Chart One.

Chart One took into account all the royal relationships I had established in the first three books, plus allowing for developments planned for the next Kelson Trilogy. Only Meraude, Nigel's wife, had not been mentioned by name, though I had plans for her in the future.

As for the far end of the Haldane line, that presented other complexities which began to sort themselves out increasingly as I worked my way through *Camber of Culdi*. By the end of the book, I was able to map out the relationships shown in Chart Two.

And so I found that the Haldane line descended from Cinhil Haldane through his fourth son, Rhys Michael Haldane and Michaela Drummond, the daughter of Cathan MacRorie's widow. But because Cinhil started his family late in life, it was inevitable that Gwynedd was slated for a succession of royal regencies; it takes a while to re-establish a royal dynasty.

At Cinhil's death, his eldest son was not quite twelve. A sickly lad, young Alroy lived only to his sixteenth year; but although he officially came of age at fourteen, he was weak and easily led, and let his regents continue to guide him. When he died and was succeeded by his twin brother Javan, it seemed apparent to all that Javan planned to reverse many of the stringent anti-Deryni policies touted by the regents during his brother's minority and thereafter, for Javan was bright and independent, and had close ties with at least one Deryni, and had good reason to distrust the former regents.

This ill-suited said regents, of course, especially with another, more pliable prince waiting in the wings, who, though he was of age, had not seen through the wiles of his brothers' former governors and who, it was expected, could be ruled by them. Javan reigned for only a year before being succeeded by the sixteen-year-old Rhys Michael Haldane, and even Rhys Michael lived only long enough to sire two sons before likewise meeting an untimely death at the age of twenty-two.

Were the deaths of both younger princes engineered by the former regents? These questions are now being answered by the Heirs of Saint Camber Trilogy.

In any case, Rhys Michael's elder son and heir, Owain, was four; and this gave the former regents a ten-year span in which to further entrench themselves and their relatives in positions of power, and to cement the anti-Deryni policies which they had begun under Alroy. Hence, in a span of nineteen years, from the death of Cinhil in 917 to the attaining of Owain's majority in 936, the regents held actual rule for twelve years and virtual rule for far more than that.

It was not until the reign of Uthyr, who was nineteen when he came to the throne and fifty-one when he died, that the Haldanes began to assert themselves and to throw off the insidious influence which had begun to be exerted even during the latter years of the reign of Cinhil Haldane—and the anti-Deryni policies would not begin to be relaxed for more than a century after that.

Uthyr's sons fared far less well than their father had. Though all three were mature men as they came to the throne, combinations of foreign and domestic warfare and sibling rivalries took their toll: Nygel, Jasher, and Cluim reigned only three, two, and nine years respectively, the first two leaving no heirs who survived their fathers. We can surmise that all of these met met violent deaths, since they all died in their mid-thirties to early forties.

Fortunately, Cluim's son was twenty by the time he came to the throne— one may surmise that perhaps he had a scholarly bent, since he would not have been groomed for the crown as the heir of the king's third son—and one may further surmise that either plague or internecine bickering claimed both him and his eldest son in 1025.

Whether Prince Cinhil tried to wrest the crown from his father prematurely, or his younger brother Malcolm tried to pit the two against one another, or a foreign war took both men, Malcolm became king at age seventeen, probably at least five years prepared, since his older brother Aidan had died in 1020. And we know something of Malcolm, grandfather of Brion, from scraps of mention in *Deryni Rising*. Both Malcolm and his son Donal Blaine lived to their mid-sixties; and Donal, father of Brion and Nigel, has tales to be told about him that will make for more than one novel in the future.

Of course, when I published this initial genealogy of the latter Haldane Kings, I was immediately swamped with questions about the first Haldanes. Was Bearand the first Haldane king? No. Then, who was?

I decided to ask Camber's daughter, Evaine, since she's my scholar and a chief source of information about early Deryni history. I knew that we would have to be dealing with the mysterious Orin, and by now I knew the dates of Orin's life (he of the *Protocols*), and so I came up with the information in Chart Three.

Evaine told the story in somewhat more detail in *Camber the Heretic*, tying in Orin and his disciple, Jodotha of Carnedd, a female Healer many years his junior. Said Evaine:

"Orin was the contemporary of Augarin, first of the Haldane kings. Augarin had two sons, Donal and Llarik. Prince Llarik, who was plotting against his father and elder brother, had Deryni in his employ. Orin knew this. So Orin sent one of his own men among Prince Llarik's men to spy....Things didn't go exactly as Orin planned.

"His man was imprisoned by Prince Llarik's men for a totally unrelated reason, and soon the prince's plot came to fruition. His brother Donal was killed in what was called a hunting accident, shot through the eye by an arrow. And Orin himself saw King Augarin die at the hands of one of Llarik's retainers.

"Llarik immediately assumed the crown, as his father's heir....Years passed....After a while, it was decided to try to avenge the death of Augarin and Donal and to oust the patricide Llarik in favor of one of his two sons, Dolon and Werrill."

Joram frowned. "But, Ryons was the next king after Llarik. Wasn't he Llarik's son?"

"I'm getting to that," Evaine replied. "The coup failed. Llarik found out about the plot and had both his sons executed as traitors. And Jodotha—"

Here Evaine faltered in her telling, a puzzled look coming across her face. "Whatever I've been remembering, the record ends here," she said. "Let's see if I can fill in the next details from history, though. Llarik was born in 651, but his sons died in 699. Prince Ryons was born the following year—but Jodotha must have died before that, or the record wouldn't end there. I wonder whether she was killed trying to protect the two princes?"

And so a whole new area of Deryni history opens up, including some information that I've glossed over in the telling, so as not to ruin *Camber the Heretic* for those who haven't read it. But it's magic of a sort, how these bits of history interweave themselves and almost take on lives of their own, suggesting plot permutations and new characters and stories. It's a discovery process as much as a creative process, and one which continues to delight and amaze me and make all the long hours behind a hot typewriter seem light and easy.

EDITOR'S NOTE

The charts appended here are reproduced exactly as constituted for their publication with the original article, and remain entirely valid. However, a few additional details have been added with the publication of subsequent books and stories in the series. These include:

King Kelson married Princess Sidana of Meara, daughter of the pretender to that throne, in 1124; she was born in 1109, and was murdered by her brother on her wedding day. Prince Conall married Rothana in 1125, and was executed later that year for treason when he tried to usurp the throne of Gwynedd. They had an unnamed son born posthumously in 1126; Conall's father Nigel decreed that his grandson would be removed from the succession and sent to an abbey for the rest of his life. Prince Nigel had a fourth child, Princess Eiran, born in 1124. King Donal was also known as Donal Blaine, presumably to distinguish him from his many-generations-removed great-uncle of the same name, the oldest son of King Augarin. Donal Blaine had a younger brother or (more probably) half-brother, Prince Richard, born about 1055, who was unmarried in 1105, aged 50 years, and probably died childless before 1120. King Bearand's name is misspelled on the chart.

Kurtz notes in her interview elsewhere in this book that siblings not in the direct line, including both princes and princesses, have been omitted from these charts until their names are mentioned in the books. She does indicate that several lines collateral to the Haldanes may exist.

CHART I
THE LATER HALDANE KINGS OF GWYNEDD

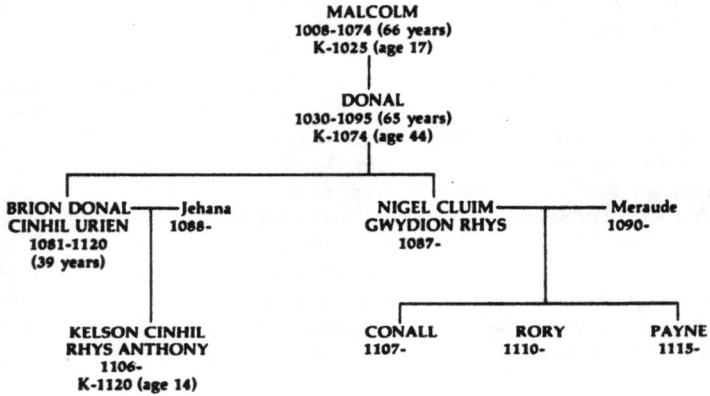

MALCOLM
1008-1074 (66 years)
K-1025 (age 17)

DONAL
1030-1095 (65 years)
K-1074 (age 44)

BRION DONAL———Jehana
CINHIL URIEN   1088-
1081-1120
(39 years)

NIGEL CLUIM———Meraude
GWYDION RHYS   1090-
1087-

KELSON CINHIL
RHYS ANTHONY
1106-
K-1120 (age 14)

CONALL   RORY   PAYNE
1107-   1110-   1115-

CHART II
THE MIDDLE HALDANE KINGS OF GWYNEDD

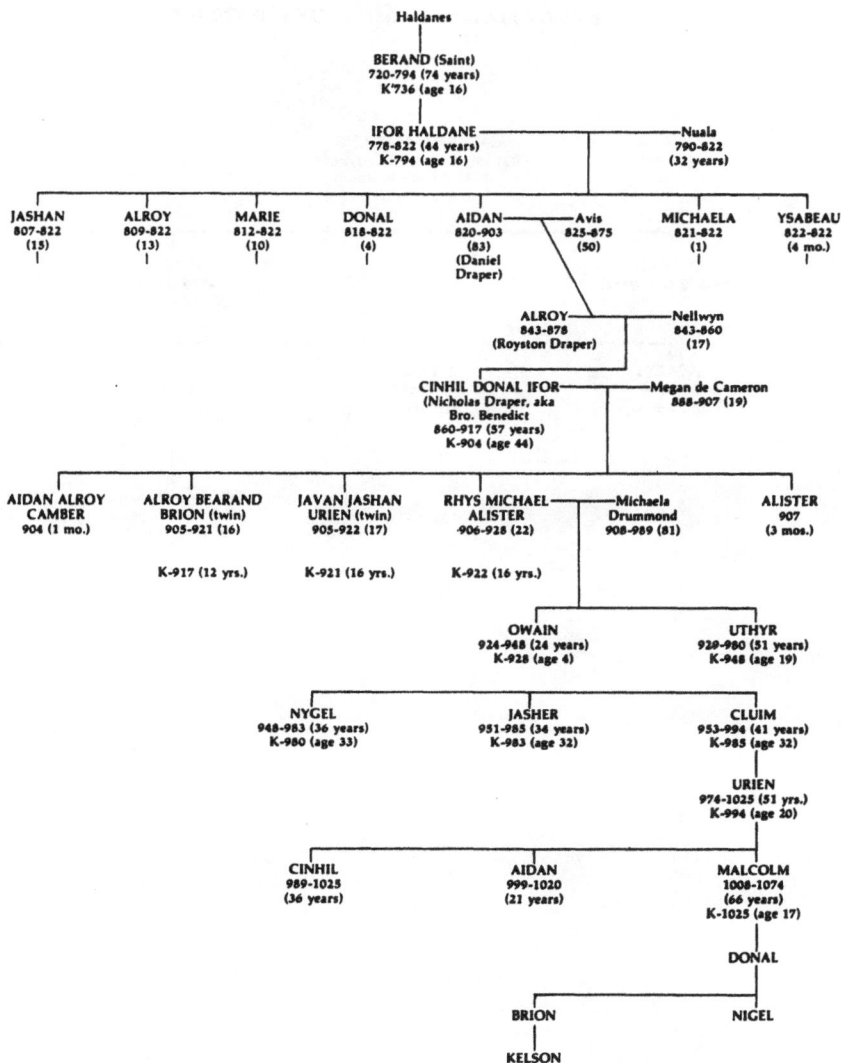

Haldanes

BERAND (Saint)
720-794 (74 years)
K'736 (age 16)

IFOR HALDANE ———— Nuala
778-822 (44 years)   790-822
K-794 (age 16)   (32 years)

JASHAN	ALROY	MARIE	DONAL	AIDAN ——— Avis	MICHAELA	YSABEAU
807-822	809-822	812-822	818-822	820-903 825-875	821-822	822-822
(15)	(13)	(10)	(4)	(83) (50)	(1)	(4 mo.)
				(Daniel Draper)		

ALROY ———— Nellwyn
843-878   843-860
(Royston Draper)   (17)

CINHIL DONAL IFOR ———— Megan de Cameron
(Nicholas Draper, aka   888-907 (19)
Bro. Benedict
860-917 (57 years)
K-904 (age 44)

AIDAN ALROY CAMBER	ALROY BEARAND BRION (twin)	JAVAN JASHAN URIEN (twin)	RHYS MICHAEL ALISTER ——— Michaela Drummond	ALISTER
904 (1 mo.)	905-921 (16)	905-922 (17)	906-928 (22) 908-989 (81)	907 (3 mos.)
	K-917 (12 yrs.)	K-921 (16 yrs.)	K-922 (16 yrs.)	

OWAIN	UTHYR
924-948 (24 years)	920-980 (51 years)
K-928 (age 4)	K-948 (age 19)

NYGEL	JASHER	CLUIM
948-983 (36 years)	951-985 (34 years)	953-994 (41 years)
K-980 (age 33)	K-983 (age 32)	K-985 (age 32)

URIEN
974-1025 (51 yrs.)
K-994 (age 20)

CINHIL	AIDAN	MALCOLM
989-1025	999-1020	1008-1074
(36 years)	(21 years)	(66 years)
		K-1025 (age 17)

DONAL

BRION	NIGEL
KELSON	

CHART III
THE EARLY HALDANE KINGS OF GWYNEDD

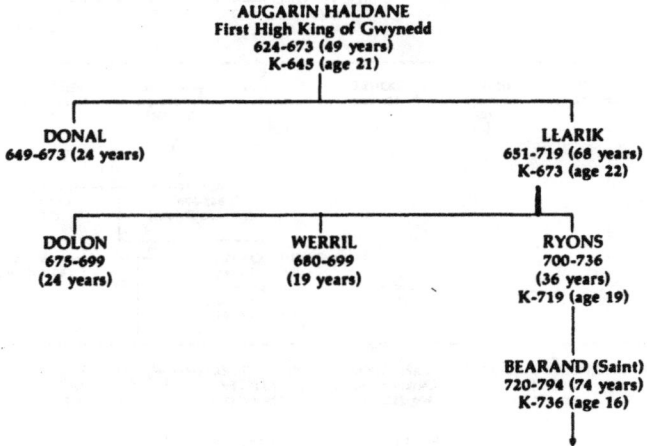

AUGARIN HALDANE
First High King of Gwynedd
624-673 (49 years)
K-645 (age 21)

DONAL
649-673 (24 years)

LEARIK
651-719 (68 years)
K-673 (age 22)

DOLON
675-699
(24 years)

WERRIL
680-699
(19 years)

RYONS
700-736
(36 years)
K-719 (age 19)

BEARAND (Saint)
720-794 (74 years)
K-736 (age 16)

TITLE INDEX

TITLE INDEX

ABOUT THE AUTHORS

BODEN CLARKE (Professor Michael Burgess) has been a librarian at California State University, San Bernardino, since 1970. The editor of the Bibliographies of Modern Authors series, he has also penned many other critiques, bibliographies, reference guides, and historical works. This is his 64th published book.

MARY A. BURGESS is the author of *The Wickizer Annals*; she has also contributed extensively to *Science Fiction and Fantasy Literature, 1975-1991*, and has edited *Across the Wide Missouri* and *The Italian Theatre in San Francisco*, among many other titles.

www.ingramcontent.com/pod-product-compliance
Lightning Source LLC
LaVergne TN
LVHW091308080426
835510LV00007B/415